The Ever Open Eye

The Ever Open Eye on the front cover was used as the divisional sign for the Guards Division in WW1 and for the Guards Armoured Division in WW2 when it was worn on the shoulder. Some years ago, whilst looking in the shop window of an outfitters in Bath, I happened to see a regimental tie with the symbol of the Ever Open Eye on it. I promptly bought it and remarked to the salesman that there must be few purchasers these days as the number of survivors dwindles.

'Oh, no,' said he. 'Only last week, an Italian bought half a dozen, because he said the ever open eye made him feel good like a gigolo.'

The Ever Open Eye

B. D. Wilson

The Pentland Press Limited
Edinburgh • Cambridge • Durham • USA

© B. D. Wilson 1998

First published in 1998 by
The Pentland Press Ltd.
1 Hutton Close
South Church
Bishop Auckland
Durham

All rights reserved.
Unauthorised duplication
contravenes existing laws.

British Library Cataloguing in Publication Data.
A Catalogue record for this book is available
from the British Library.

ISBN 1 85821 532 3

Typeset by CBS, Felixstowe, Suffolk
Printed and bound by Antony Rowe Ltd, Chippenham, Wiltshire

ACKNOWLEDGEMENTS

Some of the material in this book has already appeared in the Guards Magazine and is reproduced here by kind permission of the editor.

The maps on pages 34, 43 and 91 are reproduced by kind permission of Regimental Headquarters, Irish Guards.

CONTENTS

		Illustrations	ix
		Preface	xi
Chapter	1	Background	1
	2	Training	10
	3	Waiting	20
	4	Crossing to Normandy	22
	5	Joining the 3rd Battalion	28
	6	Learning About War	33
	7	Sourdeval	39
	8	Attack	42
	9	The Aftermath of Battle	51
	10	Filling in Time	56
	11	Advance of the Guards Armoured Division	59
	12	Entry into Brussels	68
	13	Cheerful Brussels	73
	14	Northern Belgium	78
	15	Helchteren	85
	16	Joe's Bridge	90
	17	Night Patrol	98
	18	Operation Market Garden starts	104
	19	Valkenswaard and Southern Holland	108
	20	Eindhoven and the Wilhelmina Canal	117
	21	Nijmegen	124
	22	Wounded	134
	23	American Airborne Hospital	139

24	British Casualty Clearing Station	143
25	The move to Eindhoven and Brussels	152
26	Back in England	157
27	Queen Mary's Hospital, Roehampton	164
28	On My Feet Again	170
29	Adequate Generalship?	179
30	Who Was to Blame?	183
31	Operation Market Garden Revisited	184

ILLUSTRATIONS

Memorial plaque to Irish Guards, St Charles de Percy	30
Sunken lane near Sourdeval, centre line of attack August 1944	46
Sunken lane fifty years later	47
Irish Guards in main square of Vaelkenswaard	113
Irish Guards at the approach to Nijmegen road bridge	127

MAPS

Normandy	34
Sourdeval	43
Joe's Bridge	91

Preface

This is an account of a brief undistinguished part played as an infantryman in North-West Europe in World War II. There are no heroics, no famous battles, and even less of the stirring exploits that enliven more dramatic stories. Instead, it tries to portray the day to day life of an infantry platoon commander in the Guards Armoured Division, which in September 1944 led the ground troops in Operation Market Garden. The airborne operations by British, American and Polish units from Eindhoven to Arnhem were part of the same Operation.

Although the airborne epic at Arnhem is well documented, less has been said about the failure of the Guards Armoured Division to reach Arnhem in time and the reasons for the failure. For me and possibly other members of the Division, it has been a matter of deep embarrassment that we were not able to help our airborne comrades. The blame for this needs to be laid squarely where it belongs, in the hope that future planners will not be so stupid again. It has been said, perhaps unfairly, that the Allied victory in World War II was a matter of the Axis making more mistakes than the Allies. Operation Market Garden must be reckoned as one of the bigger Allied mistakes. The aim was good but the planning unrealistic.

Early in 1945, when events were still fresh in my mind, I wrote an account of what happened to me in my military service. Hence the detailed story that follows. Without that account, I should never be able to remember all that happened over fifty years ago. It may be asked why I waited so long to put pen to paper (or finger to computer key). The answer is that, for many years after the war, I was preoccupied with my job and family, and not interested in adding to the large number of war books.

In retirement, it seemed to me a pity not to record for posterity this view of events in what was hoped to be a turning point in the war. I also felt that my family might be interested to learn what had happened to me. When veterans of World War II are now aged at least seventy and new generations come forward with less detailed knowledge of the past, it is time to set out these wartime events. I know nothing of my late father's part as an infantry Captain on the Western Front in World War I, other than that he was badly wounded in the leg. I am concerned that my family should not be left equally in the dark about myself in World War II.

Measurements are given in the Imperial scales of the day; military matters follow contemporary parlance. Neither may be in use today.

In modern peacetime, when the Footguards are resplendent on parade in full dress uniforms, it is hard to imagine wartime days in drab khaki. I never wore a bearskin or a scarlet tunic, nor did I ever possess a sword. In my day, it was battle dress, webbing belt and gaiters, boots and, for officers of the Irish Guards, a blackthorn stick on parade.

B D Wilson

Chapter 1

Background

When in 1942 the time came for me to leave school (Charterhouse), I was eager to join the Army, being then aged eighteen and anxious like my contemporaries not to miss the Second Front which had been awaited for so long. But I was advised to do two terms at Brasenose College, Oxford, which had just awarded me a Junior Hulme Exhibition, deferring my call-up to the Forces. This would ensure me a place in the College at the end of the war when demand from the backlog of Servicemen was likely to be greater than the number of places available. Reluctantly, I agreed.

Brasenose proved to be occupied by the Army, with its undergraduates farmed out to Christ Church. So I passed two terms reading Law at Oxford which by then had few undergraduates, mostly foreigners exempt from call-up, or medical students, or men like myself with deferred call-up for one reason or another. Men in the latter category were required to join the Senior Training Corps, doing two and a half days a week of basic infantry training under Guards NCOs. This was fairly intensive training that included a summer camp in the south of England.

In the summer of 1943, I left Oxford to join the Army. In the Senior Training Corps, my group had discussed our preferences and settled on the various regiments we would like to join, rather than leave it to blind fate and military vagaries. Two particular friends were keen on the 60th Rifles; a third wanted nothing but the Royal Marines (he returned after the war with a DSO awarded as a subaltern). Attracted by the Irish Guards (both my parents came from Dublin), I wrote to Regimental Headquarters in London, attended an interview with the Regimental Lieutenant-Colonel (Colonel J.S.N. Fitzgerald, who had a deformed hand from a wound in World War I), and was accepted.

At Right Flank, Pirbright Barracks in Surrey, a training depot run by the Scots Guards (Reveille was sounded by pipes, not bugles), I was put into the Brigade Squad, consisting of potential officers but currently ranked as plain guardsmen. The rest of the squad had just come from a period at the Guards Depot at Caterham, and were ahead of me in drill and barrack room procedure, but were not as fit as me (the Oxford STC had made us do lengthy run-marches every week), nor did they know much about weapon training and battle drill.

On my first day at Pirbright, we were taken for a run-march with full equipment and rifle. I had no difficulty in keeping up, but a fair-headed lad next to me kept stumbling, getting out of step, and generally showing exhaustion. Wanting to be helpful, I took his rifle as well as my own, till the Corporal came up.

'Percy. You carry your rifle and don't let me catch you again trying to get other people to help. You'll be no good in action if you can't carry your rifle.'

Later I enquired who Percy was.

'Oh, that's Lord Geoffrey Percy. His elder brother, the Duke of Northumberland, was killed in France in 1940 with the Grenadiers.'

Geoffrey sported two medal ribbons, having been a page at the Jubilee and Coronation ceremonies. More than once, an inspecting NCO on parade would yell, 'Percy. Dirty medal ribbons. Get some clean ones.' It did not seem to occur to Geoffrey that it might be simpler to leave off the medal ribbons altogether. With all the arms drill that we did, the ribbons had no hope of remaining clean for long.

The weeks passed in continual drill, weapon training, assault courses, driver training (motor cycle, 15-hundredweight and 3-ton trucks), and inspections. One day, looking out of the barrack room window, I saw a party of NCOs and another man wearing a different battledress and cap. Realising how new I was in the Army, my next door neighbour explained

The Ever Open Eye

that he was an officer, Second Lieutenant Simon Bland.

On another occasion, an NCO rushed into the communal washroom, telling us to get our shirts off quickly as the Regimental Sergeant Major was coming round and he didn't like to see men pretending to wash when they weren't stripped to the waist. I gazed in wonder at the big burly man with a splendid coat of arms taking up most of his sleeve. It was my first sighting of an RSM.

My next sighting was of Lieutenant Freddie Archer, the Quartermaster. He had previously been a legendary RSM, Scots Guards, reputed to stand to attention when speaking to an officer over the telephone. He had recently been commissioned as a QM. A group of us from the Brigade Squad were standing on the platform of Pirbright railway station one day, probably on our first weekend leave, when we saw Freddie Archer at the other end of the platform where the first class compartment of the train would normally stop. We saluted and kept our distance. To our surprise, Freddie came up and spoke to us. He sounded quite human.

At Regimental Headquarters and on other occasions, officers had warned us to do what we were told and not attempt to argue, make smart remarks, or ridicule NCOs. 'You may be potential officers but at the moment you're ordinary guardsmen, subject to normal discipline. If you step out of line, you must expect to be on a charge, and you'll have no one to blame but yourself.'

The Brigade Squad numbered about twenty, all young public school lads, bound for the five different regiments of Footguards. We varied enormously in ability. Some found no difficulty in acquiring military skills; others struggled. But the one common factor was a sense of duty. However tired or discouraged, you didn't give up. If you wanted to be a Guards officer in wartime, you had to know what you were doing and earn the respect of those you were leading. Living in a communal barrack room, you got to know the rest of the squad well. It was always apparent how hard my fellow-trainees tried (there was one exception).

The open air and exercise made us hungry. The short mid-morning break meant a rush to the NAAFI for a 'char and a wad', which translated was a cup of tea and a bun. In the mess hall, we quickly learnt that other soldiers were not above snatching food from your plate if you let your attention wander. In the barrack room, the NCOs warned us 'watch your kit'. A soldier who had lost or damaged an item of equipment might help himself to yours if you failed to take precautions. To the public school boys in the Brigade Squad, this was a new world where it paid to become street-wise as soon as possible.

The NCOs drummed into us that, in a barrack room or unit where soldiers knew each other, you had to 'muck in' and help a colleague in trouble, for instance with his equipment if he were slow in getting ready for parade. The object was to inculcate a sense of friendly solidarity which might mean the difference between life and death in action. All training was geared to what you would do when the bullets started to fly, and we all expected the Second Front (Allied invasion of Europe) to take place in the near future.

The one exception to 'mucking in' lay in cleaning your rifle for the daily inspection. Each man was required to look after his own weapon and check its serial number when he removed it from the rack for cleaning. 'What's the first step in cleaning your rifle?' the NCO would shout, and we would chorus back, 'Check its serial number.' There came the day when I failed to check properly and discovered my mistake only when I had finished cleaning the rifle and someone shouted, 'Who's taken my rifle?' To make matters worse, he flatly refused to clean mine in return, and was supported by the rest of the barrack room. It was a salutary lesson. A day or two later, a colleague who had cleaned his rifle properly was found on inspection to have something up the barrel. To his consternation, it turned out to be a spider. Ever afterwards, he was the butt of NCOs, wanting to see whether he had any more wild animals up the spout.

Towards the end of several months at Pirbright, we went by train to a camp in a wood on a ridge at Wrotham (pronounced Rootem) in Kent, to be tested for fitness to go to an Officer Cadet Training Unit (OCTU). We were tested in turn in the whole range of infantry skills, including driving. On a hill, I stalled the engine of my motor cycle and wondered gloomily whether it might mean failure. But I managed to restart successfully and take off on the hill, which satisfied the examiner. On map-reading, the Scottish officer conducting the test had laid his map case facing me so that I could read his name, Shinwell, which I recognised, his father being a leading Labour politician. To my surprise, he spent most of the time asking me what school I had attended and pointing out how superior Scottish schools were to English ones. Even so, he passed me. Some years later, I saw in a newspaper that he had gone to prison for some offence. I hoped it was a superior Scottish prison.

Wrotham was a dreadful camp, with a transient population and little attempt at providing decent facilities. The toilets consisted of a large earthenware pipe laid horizontally above the ground, with holes at intervals for you to sit on. There were no cubicles, doors, or privacy, and you supplied your own toilet paper. The tea was so bitter that it was obvious it had been doctored with bromide, in the belief that it lessened interest in sex. We were glad to see the last of the place. On our final departure by truck to the railway station at five minutes to six in the evening, we passed a group of soldiers standing outside the local pub waiting for opening time. At the head of the queue was Geoffrey Percy; he had failed the tests.

Aldershot's 161 OCTU, beside the Basingstoke Canal, was a stern world where we were rushed from one parade to the next, often with a change of uniform between. It was not uncommon to switch from battle dress to denims to physical training dress several times in the course of a morning. The OCTU took potential officers for all infantry regiments, as well as a Brigade Squad. The NCOs and officers were all from Guards regiments, with an officer for every platoon. My Platoon Commander, Lord Vaughan of the Welsh Guards, was sometimes loudly criticised on parade by the Commanding Officer. 'Lord Vaughan, what's your platoon doing over there? It should be behind No.2 platoon. I've spoken to you before about putting it in the right place.' Poor Lord Vaughan, a pleasant enough officer, would then dash up and down trying to straighten things up.

With an intake of officer cadets every month and a four months' course, there was a passing out parade every month. The cadets wore the usual battle dress uniform (blouse top, trousers, canvas gaiters, boots which were dubbined and not polished) and regimental flash on the shoulder, with a white band round the peaked service cap and the OCTU badge. There was occasional weekend leave when I would go by train up to London to stay in my mother's flat. With air raids and other unexpected delays, travel by train could be erratic. On one occasion, I arrived back late from a 36-hour pass because the train had been held up by an air raid. Placed on a charge for absence without leave, I was duly marched before the Company Commander who accepted the explanation after lecturing me on the importance of punctuality. Next day I was marched in again for being late on parade. When I explained that I was late because I had been in the Company office on a charge on the previous day and therefore could not be on parade at the same time, I could scarcely contain my amusement at the absurdity of the charge. But, mindful of discipline, I kept a straight face.

The RSM at the OCTU was the famous Tibby Brittain, Coldstream Guards, whose loud and penetrating voice would rise to a scream as he bellowed orders. It never ceased to astonish me what quick and penetrating eyes RSMs and drill sergeants possessed. Standing twenty yards away from a squad, they seldom failed to spot a soldier who had not properly done what he was required to do, whether the soldier was in the front or rear rank. The line of patter that poured out would do credit to a politician, likewise the colourful similes. 'When I say knees bend, I want you to get right down in double time . . . You at the end there . . . You look like an old lady crapping in the long grass . . . Number five in the front rank . . . You're mooning about like a pregnant nun . . . Get a hold of yourself . . . Stand closer to your razor . . . Stand straight there and look up . . . It's no good looking down at the ground for sixpences. The Scots Guards have been round here already . . . Stop laughing there.' And so it went on. The Irish Guards had their own expressions. 'Harder yet that man. Get a rift on.'

At one stage, we spent a fortnight doing nothing but night exercises, such as firing on the ranges with tracer bullets, patrolling, compass work, attack and defence. In December, we went by train to Capel Curig in

Snowdonia, Wales, for field firing exercises with live ammunition. There was a constant stream of platoon attacks up and down the mountains, firing rifles, Bren guns, and 2-inch mortars. I spoilt one attack by knocking the target over with my first burst on the Bren gun; I was never so accurate again.

Another day, with the 2-inch mortar, I was told to fire a smoke bomb. But, having loaded the bomb into the barrel, I was stopped from firing and told to move position, then ordered again to load and fire a smoke bomb. I did so and fired. The Sergeant Instructor and I watched open-mouthed as two smoke bombs sailed through the air. When in the new position I put the bomb down the barrel, I had forgotten that there was already a bomb there. If they had been high explosive and not smoke bombs, the first might have set off the second in the barrel and probably blown both our heads off. It was understood in World War II that up to 5% casualties were acceptable in field firing exercises. But, at that juncture, I was not prepared to be part of it.

It was cold in Snowdonia, with snowfalls nearly every day. One exercise had to be abandoned because the snow fell so thickly that visibility was reduced to a few yards, making it too dangerous for firing. Every time the instructors yelled 'You're under fire', we had to fling ourselves flat on wet, snowy ground, crawling and lying in it. Our clothes became soaked in no time and remained so for the two weeks that we spent in Snowdonia.

In another unarmed exercise, we were taken in groups in trucks (with the backs covered so as to prevent our seeing out) to different places and dumped there. Each group was then expected to identify where it was on the map and make its way to a particular target without being intercepted en route by staff lying in wait. The route involved crossing the Conway River which was wide and in flood. Everyone took their chance over the road bridge, except Richard Swain (we had been at school together and occupied adjoining beds in the OCTU barrack room) and another lad who was a scholar of New College, Oxford. They decided to strip and swim the river. Their dead bodies were later found downstream.

At the end of the two weeks, we were required to account for all unused ammunition; the heavy boxes of 1,252 rounds were stored in our rooms underneath the beds. We did so and signed the necessary papers, only to discover to our horror that we had overlooked one box. Worried that admission might prejudice our prospects of being commissioned, we waited till nightfall, carried the box down to a nearby bridge, and dumped it in the river. Many years later, I returned to Capel Curig and looked over the bridge into the clear waters. No sign of an ammunition box.

An important element of this battle course was training in location of fire. It is all very well flinging yourself flat when under fire, but there is no way you can fire back until you have first located where the fire is coming from. A well-concealed enemy may show little or no sign of his position, so it takes training and skill to judge where to fire back. In this respect, the traditional practice of listening for crack and thump still holds good, at any rate for single shots. The crack is caused by the sound of a bullet parting the air close to you, followed by the thump of the explosion when the weapon was fired. The trick is to ignore the crack but to listen for the thump and then judge where it came from. Not always easy. It was a revelation sometimes for the seated cadets to see the location of the Sergeant Instructor who had been firing over our heads from a concealed position and then stood up.

It was continually emphasised in training that 'cover from view isn't necessarily cover from fire'. In other words, hiding behind a bush is useless because bullets can go straight through, bearing in mind the practice of searching fire, i.e. firing at any feature where the enemy may be hiding. It was dinned into us that 'there's no divine right of commanders'. The idea that officers should walk about in the open under fire as some sort of encouragement to others was anathema. Officers were as mortal as anyone else and should take proper cover behind something solid like a rock or brick wall.

Back in Aldershot, the winter had set in, with ice and snow. We were taken one chilly morning to a nearby lake to practise the use of collapsible assault boats. To our delight, the lake was found to be covered in thick ice. We looked forward to going away and trying to get warm. At that moment, two swans flew in, landed on the ice, and skidded backwards on to their tails. Slipping and slithering, they made their way to the edge, encouraged by cheers from the frozen cadets.

To get to the closer training areas, we were required to ride bicycles, for which there was a drill. 'Stand to attention by your bicycle; hold the handlebars. Walk march. Mount and ride'. In pairs, we covered the countryside. With petrol rationing, there were very few vehicles on the roads, other than military ones. The high speed traffic these days on the Hog's Back near Aldershot is a far cry from the days in late 1943 when we cycled along there to places for map reading, fire orders, compass work, etc.

The four months of intensive training at the OCTU crammed us with knowledge, helped by little booklets issued by the Army Council on various aspects. The one that really amazed us was entitled 'The tactical handling of an armoured division in the opposed crossing of a water obstacle'. For cadets hoping to become second lieutenants, this booklet appeared to be more relevant to a divisional major-general. We assumed our promotion would be swift. The numerous permanent staff at the OCTU included ATS girls under their senior officer whom I well remember seeing a number of times in the distance. It so happened that she later married my cousin, John Allen from Dublin, who was then in the Royal Engineers and finished up a lieutenant-colonel. At the OCTU where I was but one of hundreds of cadets, she and I never met. It was years later before we met in Hong Kong where John had been posted with the Gurkha Engineers.

In due course, our Brigade Squad had its passing-out parade, and we were sent on leave before joining the Training Battalion of our respective regiments. In the meantime, we were busy arranging new service dress from the approved tailors. The uniform was made of a fine baratea cloth, beautifully cut and stitched, with four buttons on the cuff for the Irish Guards. In addition to the khaki service cap, there was a blue dress cap with gold braid on the brim, a Sam Browne belt, a blackthorn stick and a battle-dress with faced lapels. The half dozen new second lieutenants in my intake joined the Training Battalion, IG, at Hobbs Barracks, Lingfield, in Surrey.

Chapter 2

Training

Joining the Training Battalion was like being a new boy at school. Apart from the psychological difference of now being an officer and no longer a guardsman, there was the problem of finding one's feet and acquiring self-confidence in a completely new environment. This was not helped by the then Guards convention that, in the Mess, second lieutenants (ensigns) should be largely ignored.

Not until they became lieutenants (in World War II, after six months) did other officers bother to talk to them. In the case of sons of important well-known people, some notice might be taken for the first fortnight, but thereafter the cold treatment crept in. The object of this was apparently to make clear that in the modern Army it was military, not social, rank that counted. There was a saying that 'X was a very kindly officer. He used to talk to ensigns'. Fortunately, with half a dozen new officers in our intake, we could talk to each other and were therefore self-sufficient. All had Irish connections, including Dick Nelson-Bobbet, a British Latin-American Volunteer (BLAV) from Buenos Aires who, as a conscript in the Argentine, had earlier served in the Argentine cavalry as a groom. Older than the rest of us, he was a fund of racy stories and romantic experiences that kept his innocent listeners wide-eyed with envy.

We were at once put on a Young Officers course, going through the range of military skills all over again. This time it was in company with corporals under training. We fired every infantry weapon (including German ones) in the local ranges. We threw grenades in Godstone chalk pits. We marched and ran miles in battle order. We set off explosives on Lingfield racecourse (no racing during the war). We practised covering fire and attack, with each of us in turn firing the Bren with live ammunition, whilst the remainder advanced nervously at right angles towards the fire, hoping that the gunner would stop in time. On one occasion, we were required to advance in line abreast, each firing a Bren from the hip. As we advanced, there was an explosion beside me, causing the Corporal Instructor on my right to collapse with numerous injuries. Some unit (not a Guards one) had left an unexploded 69 grenade which the unfortunate Corporal had knocked with his foot. He recovered after a few weeks.

Part of Guards standards and training was an insistence that no unexploded ordnance should be left behind. Corporal Jimmy Rioch, a huge tough in the Scots Guards, who was reputed to have been a pre-war bayonet fighting champion, dinned this into us at Pirbright, where we watched him throwing stones and finally shooting at an unexploded grenade. After every firing exercise, we were required to pick up the empty cartridge cases, for recycling. Before leaving any area that we had occupied (even for lunch), we were always sent round the area to pick up all rubbish, ensuring that the place was left clean and tidy. The efficiency of a unit could often be judged by the condition of any area vacated by it.

We were introduced to the drill for blackthorn sticks which officers were required to carry on parade: in the right hand when marching but to be transferred rapidly to the left hand when halting or about to salute. There were of course occasions when the left hand failed to catch the stick on transfer, with the result that the stick flew across the parade ground.

Because of frequent air raid warnings at night, a captain and an ensign were placed on duty every night, to turn out when the warning was sounded to fight fires and generally organise relief if the camp was bombed. During the Young Officers course, it was my turn. But, worn out by the daily exertions, I failed to hear the air raid warning, and woke up only when I heard a guardsman outside the hut calling me. I dressed hurriedly and went to the assembly point, to be met by an angry captain who flashed a torch straight in my face and kept it there, demanding to know why I was late and why I was not wearing a tie. There was a lot more abuse. What irritated me was that all this was conducted in front of a knot of guardsmen.

Next morning, I marched myself in before the Adjutant who shared an office with the Commanding Officer, and laid a complaint about the Captain, ensuring that my voice was loud enough for the CO to hear every word. The Adjutant gave me no sympathy at all, telling me to go away and stop whining. That evening a major told me that the Captain had been reprimanded. So I gained my point after all.

The Adjutant was not a likeable person. One weekend when a couple of us were not required for duty, the Adjutant refused our applications for weekend leave. A colleague therefore drove a Bren carrier out of the camp to the railway station, with the rest of us crouching down out of sight on the floor of the carrier.

At the end of the Young Officers course, I was made a weapon training instructor for a batch of new guardsmen who appeared to be largely English ex-policemen. Apart from a sizeable number of volunteers from Northern and Southern Ireland (no conscription in either country), the remaining guardsmen tended to have Irish connections, often being first or second generation migrants to Britain. But, by early 1944, the need to bring regiments up to strength before the Second Front led to much posting without regard to ethnic background. Although I quite enjoyed the period, it was largely physical, with little demand on the brain. I shared a room with John Blake, who specialised in explosives with the Pioneer Platoon. On one occasion, I was about to put my boots in the cupboard when he said, 'Oh, do be careful. I've put some guncotton and detonators in there, but it's quite safe as they're separate from each other'. I insisted on their removal. Instructors in explosives loved to demonstrate that guncotton would not explode unless subject to a detonating wave, in the form of a detonator inserted into the guncotton with a fuse attached. The demonstration usually meant cutting off a piece of guncotton with a pocket-knife and lighting it with a match, whilst holding the cut-off piece in the hand.

Whilst taking a lengthy run-march one day, I remarked to a weary guardsman beside me, 'Oh, listen. There's a nightingale singing.' He looked round at me without enthusiasm but was too well trained to say anything. But I could see in his eyes and expression what he felt. 'Here am I dead beat after ten miles, and all the bloody officer can do is talk to me about nightingales.' He would be lucky if he heard one there today.

Parades, training marches and formed movement were usually carried out to music from the uniformed pipers playing Irish tunes. The pipers were trained guardsmen (not musicians) whose operational role was to act as stretcher-bearers. In those days, the pipes had two drones in the Irish tradition. Now, with the passion for standardisation, they follow the Scottish pattern of three drones.

On weekend leave in London, I was walking down Regent Street when I met a young Scots Guard's ensign wearing his blue cap. He was obviously Chinese. Rumour had it that he was Marshal Chiang Kai-Shek's son-in-law. (The Marshal was Generalissimo of Nationalist China.)

All this came to an end in April 1944 when I was posted to the operational 3rd Battalion, Irish Guards, at Malton in Yorkshire. At this stage in the war, the IG had only one infantry service battalion, the 1st Battalion having been severely depleted in Tunisia and Anzio. (The 2nd Battalion was an armoured one.) Life in the 3rd Battalion was more relaxed than at the Training Battalion. These were all trained soldiers waiting for the action to start. At a big exercise on the Yorkshire moors, when every weapon was fired, I heard for the first time the sound of 25-pounder artillery shells whining overhead from guns in the rear. At the conclusion of the exercise, I was talking to a fusilier in the Northumberland Fusiliers, the machine-gun regiment with the Guards Armoured Division, of which the 3rd Battalion formed part. I had not met a Northumberland accent before and he could hardly understand what I was saying either, much to the amusement of the nearby guardsmen.

On a Sunday morning in Malton, I and a few other young officers (some of whom were new to me) had a pleasant drink in the Green Man pub where I was introduced to Lieutenant John Luxembourg (Prince John).

In 1940 when Luxembourg was invaded, he and his parents (Grand Duke and Duchess) had been evacuated from Luxembourg and, in Britain, he had joined the Irish Guards. He is now Colonel of the Regiment and Grand Duke of Luxembourg. We met again many years later in Hong Kong.

A letter from Robert Neild, who had been at school with me, revealed that he was in hospital at York with a kidney complaint. So I took a bus into York at the weekend, found my way to the hospital and eventually reached him in an Other Ranks ward. (He was an aircraftsman second class in the RAF.) It was a splendid reunion.

This period ended with the whole battalion moving by train to a destination which we were not allowed to know until we got there. This meant hours of peering out of the windows whenever we passed through a station to try and see one of the few name boards still left after the invasion scare of 1940 when there was wholesale removal of name boards. Our destination turned out to be Eastbourne in Sussex where we occupied requisitioned bungalows. The south of England at this stage was crammed full of troops and equipment waiting for the Second Front. Fortunately, with Allied air superiority, German bombing of the obvious targets was minimal.

On the other hand, almost every night we could hear the sound of Allied bombing raids on the other side of the Channel, over 100 miles away. There would be a continuous rumbling roar, with the windows rattling.

In case of German air raids, we were required to dig slit trenches in the gardens of the bungalows. This was none too easy through the underlying chalk. Wielding a pick one day, I hammered at the chalk and made some progress until there came a brilliant flash and low explosion. The point of the pick melted. I had chopped through a concrete cover over an electricity cable, both being unrecognisable under a coating of chalk dust. Only the wooden handle of the pick had saved me from electrocution. In due course, a workman arrived from the electricity company. I explained that someone had cut through the cable by mistake. He went away to do something and, on his return, said, 'You must have been digging pretty hard to smash the concrete like that. We have enough of a job without people like you adding to it.' I departed rapidly elsewhere.

I shared a room in Eastbourne with Pod Bourke (Patrick O'Donnell Bourke), a tall bespectacled lad who liked to sing 'I dream of Jeanie with the light brown hair'. We were fellow platoon commanders in No.2 Company under Major Anthony Eardley-Wilmot, an experienced long-serving officer.

After only a fortnight, William Harvey-Kelly and I were sent with a party of guardsmen to a tented camp near Aldershot in Hampshire, to act as reinforcements to fill vacancies as casualties occurred in the 3rd Battalion after the opening of the Second Front. We tried to keep the men busy but it was a hard job, with too many units competing for the few training areas. Every heath and wood in Hampshire and Surrey seemed to be either occupied as a camp or used as a training area. Looking at their protected growth today, it is hard to visualise the sandy wastes of 1944, with ground torn up by tracked vehicles, broken trees, patches of oil and diesel, and signs of military activity everywhere.

I was once instructed to be duty officer overnight for the guard at a nearby camp for military prisoners. The guard consisted of soldiers from non-Guards units. The camp turned out to be a barbed-wire enclosure sited on heathland, with several dozen prisoners awaiting court martial and meanwhile sleeping under rough shelters, with pit latrines and wooden troughs for washing. All this was out in the open, with no perimeter lighting (wartime blackout in force). Most of the prisoners were apparently to be charged with absence without leave or desertion.

As the expected Second Front loomed closer, desertions became more frequent from soldiers unwilling to become involved. I was reminded of an incident weeks earlier on returning late in the evening by train to Aldershot. There were shouts from behind the press of soldiers making for the exit, and a hatless figure scuttled past me dodging round the crowd like a startled hare, pursued by a couple of equally rapid Military Policemen.

In probably every war where there is conscription, not every serviceman or woman wishes to be placed in a position of danger, but is prepared to go absent or desert at some stage. To curb this pattern, the military authorities require a police force, holding camps, legal processes, and prisons. It is not an edifying picture and certainly not one to compete with traditional death or glory.

A Military Policeman at the camp told me of a rumour that there might be a break-out that night. Before it grew dark, I thought it better to check the perimeter and familiarise myself with the position of sentries, any dead ground, and possible weak points in the fence. As I started to walk round, a crowd of prisoners kept pace with me on the inside of the wire, keeping up a running commentary:

''Ere, 'oo let you outta the nursery?'

'Where's yer mum, little boy? She'll want to know why you aren't at school.'

'Oh, don't be nasty to 'im. 'E'll wet his pants.'

When a shower of stones landed round me, lobbed over the top of the 12-foot high fence, I began to be slightly worried. At that point, a voice from near my feet said, 'I'd get down here, if I were you, sir.' It was a sentry standing down a slit trench. I took his advice. It was apparently necessary for sentries to take shelter much of the time. Eventually I managed to complete the circuit and decide on tactics.

Although all sentries were armed with rifles and live ammunition (myself with a .38 Smith and Wesson revolver), I gave orders that there should be no firing under any circumstances. Each sentry must be provided with a whistle. If trouble started, he must blow his whistle repeatedly and use his bayonet on prisoners trying to escape. (If he shot a prisoner, he might have difficulty justifying it afterwards, whereas bayonet wounds could possibly be attributed to barbed wire.) I emphasised that, if a sentry failed to use his bayonet, he ran the risk of a desperate prisoner seizing his rifle and shooting the sentry.

I lay fully dressed on my camp bed in the guard room, and was woken in the early hours by whistles. I rushed out to find a sentry had obeyed instructions to the letter, having prodded a number of would-be escapers through the wire with his bayonet. There was much shouting and abuse from within the enclosure.

In the morning, when my tour of duty finished at 6 am, I returned to camp across the heath, losing my way a couple of times in a thick ground mist. Sitting at breakfast, I was summoned by the alarmed Camp Commandant to say that two prisoners had escaped at 6.30 am by wriggling through the bottom of the fence, which they had lined with clothing to protect them from the barbs, and could not be tracked because of the mist. Since the escape took place after I had properly stood down, I was in the clear and returned thankfully to breakfast.

Next morning I was ordered to act as prosecuting officer at a court martial in Aldershot. Having only the vaguest idea of what was needed, I attended earlier than my stated time, to watch proceedings at a couple of other courts martial; they seemed to be almost non-stop performances. This was hardly surprising, bearing in mind the camp of prisoners that I had just been guarding.

My case involved an unhappy private soldier charged with absence without leave, possibly desertion. Hearing that his wife was believed to be carrying on with someone else, he had gone absent and spent days hanging round his house, watching the prolonged visits of a stranger, but had himself never entered the house nor confronted his wife. He had then been picked up by Military Police, who would naturally go first to his home address.

I have always felt remorse that I showed the accused no mercy. At that stage, I had insufficient experience of life to appreciate that the man may have been beside himself with worry, confused and uncertain what to do, possibly nervous of tackling his wife, and frightened of returning to his unit after an unauthorised absence. He should, of course, have taken his problem to his Company Commander in the first place, but not everyone does the right thing all the time. In accordance with court martial procedure in those days, I was excluded from the court when the decision was handed down, and so remain ignorant to this day about what happened to the soldier. It seemed to me ridiculous that, in civil law, counsel for both sides were allowed to remain in court for the verdict, but not so in this particular court martial.

Near our camp was a camp of Canadian soldiers. I passed them one chilly day carrying out an assault crossing of a small canal. Loud cries of anguish filled the air as they charged through ice and freezing water, to emerge dripping on the other side. After crossing the Atlantic, many had spent a year or two sitting around in Britain, waiting to be called upon for a Second Front. They were not required for the North African Campaign at all. It must have been a trying and frustrating period.

Cycling from Charterhouse one summer's day, I had stopped at the side of the road to watch a group of soldiers levelling a field. Chatting to them, they turned out to be Canadian Engineers creating an airfield in six weeks.

'Who's in charge?' I asked.

'Oh, that'll be Al. He's over there driving the bulldozer. He's a captain.'

Al was stripped to the waist, covered in dust, with a handkerchief tied over his nose.

Whilst at the Training Battalion in Lingfield, Johnnie Gough and I had taken the train to London one weekend. The third class appeared to be full, but we had a first class compartment to ourselves. Presently the door opened and a smiling Canadian soldier entered, saying that there was no room in the third class and he hoped we would not mind if he sat with us in first. I was prepared to tell him to go away, but Johnnie Gough was more democratic and invited him to stay. The Canadian never stopped talking, with a fund of stories about the scrapes that boredom had led him into, including his periods in the 'glasshouse' (military prison). A most astonishing character, with none of the class-consciousness that tended in those days to surround British and Continentals.

Whilst I was undergoing driver training at Pirbright, we had occasion to go to Midhurst. In a pub there one evening, amidst a crowd of soldiers, a Canadian apparently the worse for wear had placed his head on the table and seemed to be asleep. Presently he stood up and, with his eyes shut, sang 'Annie Laurie' in a magnificent tenor voice. The crowd fell silent and listened spellbound; they may have heard him before. Tumultuous cheers when he finished and went back to sleep.

Canadian soldiers were usually better dressed than their British counterparts, with uniforms that fitted well. It looked as if every Canadian unit had its own tailor who was kept busy. There was none of the baggy appearance of British soldiers issued with standard sizes of uniform that too often failed to take account of individual proportions. Where, for instance, two men were of equal height, one might have longer legs but shorter arms than the other, but they both received the same size of uniform. A tailor was needed to put matters right, and it was noticeable that Canadians (and American forces too) seemed to do just that. Needless to say, every Guards battalion had its own tailor.

It was during this period at the reinforcement camp near Aldershot that a message came round to say that the great Joe Louis, the then reigning world heavyweight boxing champion, would be giving an exhibition bout. Eager to see this demonstration, I went to the appointed place, to find hundreds of other interested fans (British and American servicemen) crowding round an open-air boxing ring that was fortunately set high above the few spectators in seats and the rest standing behind. An enormous coloured man in a shiny purple dressing gown, with Methuselah written across the back, clambered into the ring and proceeded to don a brown leather helmet and boxing gloves. He was followed by Joe Louis himself who appeared quite short compared to his sparring partner, although the champion stood in fact well over six feet tall.

The two took off their dressing gowns and came hopping and twitching into the middle of the ring where the master of ceremonies introduced them to the crowd, explaining that the sparring partner's helmet was not for his own protection but to prevent damage to the champion's hands.

For several rounds, the pair boxed to cheers from the crowd, although it was all too obvious that there was nothing serious in the bout; just a training session, with Methuselah back-pedalling much of the time and acting as a punch-bag for the champion's punches which came at astonishing speed. For a big man, he was surprisingly light on his feet.

For myself and most of the other spectators, it was probably the only time in our lives that we could see a heavyweight boxing champion in live action, and it took a war to bring this about. Much too difficult in peacetime.

Chapter 3

Waiting

Once again, William Harvey-Kelly and I were on the move, with a group of guardsmen. This time, it was to a tented camp in a sandy desolation at Bordon in Hampshire, run by some other unit. There were reinforcements there for other Guards regiments, including the IG, one of whom enraged some line regiment officers in the mess by wearing his cap to breakfast (an IG practice). A fellow Coldstream officer was the Marquis of Hartington, later killed in Belgium.

The Camp Commandant (a line regiment officer) was dismayed one day to discover that a group of Irish Guardsmen was charged with mutiny in the camp. Apparently, an unpopular and unfeeling sergeant had been taking a drill parade. Over a period of time, he must have irritated the guardsmen so much that, before the parade, they had agreed amongst themselves to stand fast and ignore commands. Technically, where five or more soldiers refuse to obey a lawful order, they can be charged with mutiny. There may well have been extenuating circumstances here and, in more settled conditions, the situation ought never to have occurred. Officers should have seen the danger signs and taken action accordingly, but in the coming and going of the reinforcement camp at Bordon they were not recognised. More is the pity. Soldiers should never be goaded beyond endurance.

Shortly afterwards, I was duty officer and visited a prisoner, an Irish Guardsman, in his stockade, a small wired enclosure with no roof. Wanting to speak to the prisoner, I asked the Sergeant to open the padlocked door, so as to avoid my having to speak through the wire. 'I wouldn't go inside, sir. He might attack you.'

Addressing the prisoner, I asked, 'Will you attack me?'

The prisoner, who had stood up on my approach and was therefore still aware of normal behaviour towards an officer, answered 'No, sir, I wouldn't do that.'

So I entered the enclosure. He looked bewildered and miserable, as indeed he might be.

'Where do you sleep?'

'There, sir, on the ground,' pointing to a single blanket on the sand.

I was horrified at this treatment of a soldier, not yet convicted of any crime and treated like an animal. 'Get him a camp bed, Sergeant, and another blanket, too. He's entitled to better conditions than these.'

This was unusual. Generally guardsmen were looked after and fed well, with company sergeant majors expected to keep their ears to the ground and report any signs of dissatisfaction before trouble gained ground. Discipline was firm ('check all faults all the time') but fair. The aim was not to stifle all initiative and common sense so that a man could not think for himself in the absence of orders, but rather to instil standards of military skill that would come to the fore in the heat of battle. Training was hard, and so was play. My only complaint was the tradition (certainly in the IG) that manliness came out of a bottle. There seemed to be far too much emphasis on drinking alcohol. Even at that early age, and despite my willingness to follow suit, I felt that a change in attitude might be no bad thing.

Aircraft with their radial engines droned overhead much of the day and part of the night too. Early on the morning of 6 June 1944, as I emerged from my tent to wash and shave in a canvas bucket, the sky was filled with aircraft and gliders. There was a general shout and cheering as men poured from their tents, realising that the Second Front had been opened and the long wait for action was nearly over. But it was near the end of July before William and I and parties of guardsmen from other regiments were on our way.

Chapter 4

Crossing to Normandy

We were six officers, with about 150 men. The column staggered down the road to the station, laden with large packs, small packs, weapons, and all sorts of equipment. The train to Newhaven on the south coast took a long time, stopping and starting. Aldershot station, with its solid Victorian architecture, had been dreary in the early morning. At the best of times, in 1944, the town bore all the evidence of an overcrowded profession. Troops, troops, nothing but troops. (I once saw three civilians together.) Newhaven looked little better. The railhead was almost at the side of the estuary, with every inch crammed with equipment. The embarkation staff seemed highly efficient in their monotonous job of transferring bodies from trains to ships, although it must at times have sorely taxed their patience.

There was usually some fool who, in the excitement of the moment, drops his steel helmet into the sea or leaves his rifle behind on the platform. To compound matters, the staff were not themselves handling the men but through the officers of the draft, and the officers were often quite busy enough humping their own kit or counting the men. We hung about the docks uncomfortably, herded together on a disused railway platform.

The ubiquitous tea urn turned up; the NAAFI vehicle dispensed char and wads whilst the temporary latrine did a thriving business. A padre wandered round to settle minds and problems. Another individual shouted warnings of what would happen to you if you took English money out of the country: 'Your last chance! Your last chance! Change your English money into francs.' He was like a racecourse bookie. (The francs were specially printed in Britain for use in France by the BLA.)

Finally, in the late afternoon, the mass of khaki was ordered up, shouldered its kit, and marched up the quayside to be checked against the nominal roll on a ship sheet, before making its way to its allotted Landing Ship Infantry. In our case, this meant clambering across three other LSIs moored alongside each other; army boots are not the best footwear for walking on steel plates, still less when you are unbalanced with heavy equipment on your back. The men were placed in a large hold containing wooden benches; the officers in a small hold at the stern beside the engines.

At the quayside we had been issued with inflatable Mae West life belts. Mine was covered in sand, dried salt crystals, and bits of seaweed. We were also given three greaseproof paper seasick bags. Expecting irregular meals at the other end, I filled mine with biscuits.

It was an overcast day, with a strong breeze, but reasonably calm in the Newhaven estuary. But as soon as we cleared the estuary, in company with the three other LSIs, and reached the open English Channel, the breeze became a gale with rough seas. The ship rolled, pitched and tossed. Guardsmen on deck clung on like limpets. I wedged myself firmly on the platform of an Oerlikon gun.

It was not long before a corporal was sick over the side, followed by an increasing number of others. Once the ship made an effort to turn back but then changed its mind and resumed its original course, with a feeble groan from seasick guardsmen. The misery continued through the night for fifteen hours. Feeling terrible, I retired below and was promptly sick, not even having time to remove the biscuits. Each time I came on deck to throw another bag over the side, an enormous Welsh Guards sergeant would grin and invite me to share one of the sandwiches that he was constantly eating.

The morning dawned more calmly with the coast of France on the horizon. The ship crawled in past floating debris of every description, to tie up alongside a huge concrete caisson of Mulberry Harbour opposite the town of Arromanches. Floated across the Channel, a dozen or so caissons had been sunk several hundred yards offshore, connected to the shore by single-lane floating pontoons. The harbour contained all sorts of vessels: tankers, landing craft, destroyers, motor torpedo boats, etc. A tank-landing ship with its bow doors open disgorged a steady stream of 3-ton trucks, which manoeuvred over ramps and round obstructions with remarkable skill for drivers who might not have been feeling their best after the rough sea crossing.

As soon as they reached shore, vehicles drove on the right of the road. When the Guards contingent disembarked, I was still so seasick that the ground seemed to be moving although I was standing on a solid concrete caisson resting on the sea bottom. William Harry-Kelly marched the men over the pontoon during a break in the traffic, leaving me to take charge of the baggage which was loaded on a truck. I blessed him for this arrangement, as I could not have marched an inch with my large pack on my back.

The truck bounced over the pontoon, passing an amphibious DUKW in the water laden with ammunition boxes. As we neared the shore, we met the first of the notices that said 'Drive fast'. The pontoons ended at the foot of a small cliff which was broken down to form a ramp paved with wire netting. The truck accelerated safely up the slope; not so several trucks which had earlier failed to make the grade and now lay on either side abandoned.

We caught up our marching contingent lying sprawled in a sloping field, unshaven and haggard. After a suitable rest, we set off on foot to find our camp. It turned out to be a warm day and the dust lay thickly everywhere. Being late July, the summer was in full bloom. No one could direct us to this camp. We passed ruined villages, taciturn Normans, and trailing telephone wires from concrete pylons.

At one stage, we stopped beside a cornfield where a pair of horses towed an ancient reaper round a diminishing patch of wheat. A rabbit bolted from the patch, whereupon the farmer on the seat of the reaper was galvanised into action. Yelling blue murder, he leapt to the ground, scaring the horses into a particularly crooked swathe of corn. He was joined by a group of children who raced across the stubble and all pursued the rabbit. The din and excitement were terrific. The rabbit dived under a bale of straw, where it was bludgeoned to death, and the farmer appeared triumphantly carrying the rabbit by the ears. The guardsmen enjoyed this hugely. The sporting school shouted encouragement, whilst the potential animal liberators demanded fair play.

After some five miles, we eventually discovered the temporary staging camp which had apparently moved on the previous day from elsewhere. The camp consisted of tents erected over circular holes in the ground. In the evening, I strolled out with William to look at the nearest village. It was a handful of well-preserved houses that seemed now to act as a handy background for military notice-boards. Every inch was placarded with arrows to Bayeux, Caen, the beaches, 101 Reinforcement Group, Nth petrol dump, local ammunition supply, water point, HQs, etc.

The roads carried a never-ending stream of vehicles going to and from the front which at that stage was perhaps some twenty miles away. What struck me so much in the beach-head was the sense of urgency and the need to hurry, to build up men and supplies before the enemy became strong enough to hurl the invaders back into the sea. The traffic started in the early morning and stopped only when it grew too dark. There was little or no driving at night, presumably because of the blackout and danger of showing lights and inviting air attack. Every inch of the beach-head seemed to be filled with troops, equipment and supplies. It was an absolute hive of activity, well regulated and efficiently organised.

On my first night, I slept like a log until the early hours of the morning when I awoke to the thunder of guns, a roar of aeroplanes, the explosion of bombs, and a brilliant display of tracer in the sky. Splashes of colour from Bofors anti-aircraft guns would burst in vertical line upwards towards the German aircraft. William and I were worried about the shell splinters likely to be raining down from the anti-aircraft fire. The shallow footings of the tents and the canvas roof offered no protection. There was a continual patter of objects on the roof but strangely enough no holes in the canvas. It was not till next morning that we discovered the falling objects to be apples dislodged by concussion from the tree above us. There were apple orchards all over Normandy, with lovely red apples at this season. Sadly, as many a guardsman discovered to his cost, they were not eating apples but bitter-tasting cider apples.

We set off again at about midday in search of another more permanent reinforcement camp outside Bayeux. The roads were so narrow and the traffic so heavy that we moved in single file, on the left of the road to face the oncoming traffic. The dust rose like a mist over the face of the sea, aggravated by the fact that few roads boasted tarmac surfaces; most consisted of pavé, small stones set in earth. The dust never had time to settle but rose thicker with every vehicle that passed. I was never so choked with dust as in Normandy. It caught the back of your throat till you gasped for breath. Your face was coated with a yellow film. Beneath trousers, gaiters, socks and boots, your feet and ankles turned black. Sometimes the dust lay so thickly underfoot, particularly where tracked vehicles had churned the surface, that a column of marching soldiers made no sound. For despatch riders on motor cycles, it was even worse. Apart from not being able to see the road ahead clearly, their goggles needed to be wiped continuously, and a scarf across the nose and face was essential.

Our new camp, which held reinforcements for the five Guards regiments, lay astride a tarmac road just outside Bayeux, where we lived in tents for a week in the usual orchard, waiting till the 3rd Battalion required replacements, i.e. dead men's shoes. During the day, we devised schemes to keep the guardsmen occupied and amused. There were several dumps of German equipment nearby, so William and I first experimented to see how the weapons and ammunition worked before giving a series of demonstrations. From training, everyone knew the sound of fire from British small-arms, but it was desirable that we should also be familiar with the sound of German small-arms and how to fire them, too.

One day Frankie, who was now in charge of us, decided that it would be a good idea to march to the coast and have a swim, if only to get rid of the dust. Unfortunately, although the weather before and after was hot and sunny, coast-day was overcast, cold and windy. With our pipes playing, we marched the seven miles or so to the coast. As we drew nearer, the ravages of war became more apparent. The village nearest the sea was just a heap of rubble. The fields there were devoid of all vegetation; just a mass of shell and bomb holes and displaced earth. We scrambled down a collapsed part of the cliff above the beach, keeping within the white tapes and the German notices of 'Achtung. Minen.' At the bottom, we clambered over an upturned landing craft and faced a cold, uninviting sea whipped by a keen onshore breeze. William and I did our duty in the chilly sea, but few of the men followed suit, claiming that they did not know how to swim. One sturdy lad swam out and returned with a floating rum jar. But his luck ran out when it was found to be empty.

Every day, friends in other regiments were drafted off to their battalions, leaving the two IG officers on their own. I attempted to teach my batch of men some elementary French but met trouble when told, 'But, sir, Prince John said it was something else.'

In the afternoons and evenings, we did the rounds of Bayeux which was quite undamaged. The first stop was the cathedral and the tapestry. The original Bayeux tapestry had been removed for safekeeping some time before and was replaced by a replica. It was an astonishing sight to see the cathedral full of troops of various regiments and corps wandering round, all carrying rifles and other weapons. You were required to carry arms outside your camp. The streets of the town were full of troops walking up and down, quietly looking at the sights. For most, it was their first taste of the Continent. There was no entertainment, as the military population was transient. There was a ban on the purchase of practically every article in French shops, for fear that there would not be enough for the French inhabitants themselves. The officers mess had earlier acquired a stock of Camembert cheese made locally. (There was a smelly, disused cheese factory down the road.) It came in the traditional round wooden boxes, varying in consistency and odour.

Emerging from the cathedral one day, I was faced by a column of tanks and vehicles thundering through the narrow street, forcing me to take shelter in a doorway. This turned out to be the Polish Armoured Division newly landed at Mulberry Harbour and anxious to get to the front. They were a long way from home.

Chapter 5

Joining the 3rd Battalion

On 3 August we were ordered to proceed to the 3rd Battalion. My servant had been drafted two days earlier as a rifleman, much to his disgust. He complained bitterly that, as he had been a storeman for the previous two and a half years and so was out of practice as an ordinary platoon member, he might as well write on his wooden cross now and bring it with him. Exaggeration, of course. A trained guardsman is unlikely to forget his military skills. Laden down as usual, we embussed in troop carrying vehicles (big 4-wheel drive open-sided lorries with a canvas roof, carrying a platoon in the back on benches) in a column with an RASC officer in the leading vehicle.

We set off in fine style on a tarmac road but after a while the engine of my TCV spluttered and died. The TCVs behind stopped, too, but the vehicles in front disappeared ahead. This left me in an agony of apprehension, as I did not know the way to where we were supposed to be going. Fortunately, after fiddling for a moment or two, my RASC driver realised that his petrol tank was empty and that he had forgotten to switch over to the reserve tank. On the move once more, we raced ahead on the tarmac road to catch up the column. As the miles and the hours passed, we seemed to get no nearer our destination. The tarmac ended; the dust rose from unpaved roads which sometimes consisted of stretches of channel tracking through fields and hedges.

At midday, we reached a kind of forward reception centre where a good meal awaited us. Then on again into the dust and potholes.

Occasionally we found squads of Pioneers stripped to the waist and burnt dark by the sun, attempting to repair the road. In the late afternoon, right in the centre of Normandy in the bocage country, we reached A Echelon of the 3rd Battalion (dealing with administrative and immediate supply matters), in the village of St Charles de Percy. It was a countryside of woods and hills, thick hedges, and fields. Just beyond, in the inevitable orchard, lay the battalion itself, weary and dirty. I may have been dusty and dishevelled, but at least I sported a collar and tie and a crease in my trousers.

When I met Pod Bourke, he wore a face veil in place of a tie, with his steel helmet on the back of his head. 'Just been burying Thomas,' he said. 'Bad business. Walked into a Spandau. You'll be taking over his platoon. Ellis was killed the other day, too. Stood too long in a gap.' (Thomas was Lieutenant Thomas Stafford-King-Harmon. Ellis was Captain Ellis Woods, second in command of No.2 Company.) William and I saw the Commanding Officer (Lieutenant-Colonel J.O.E. Vandeleur); 'The situation is that we had a battle yesterday and today we're sitting in reserve.' Our indoctrination was completed by a visit to Major Anthony Eardley-Wilmot commanding 2 Company.

As I crossed the road to join my platoon, I passed a broken Spandau in the ditch surrounded by belts of ammunition and their metal carrying-box. The platoon seemed to recognise me from my previous posting in the 3rd Battalion in Malton, Yorkshire. They were dug in well in slit trenches round a farm and, at this hour in the evening, on the prowl to scrounge food. The mortar man offered me half a chicken and was surprised when I said I was not hungry.

Inevitably, I had some difficulty in knowing how to run things, bearing in mind that I was a newcomer in a platoon that had been in action for weeks. There were quite a lot of remarks such as 'Uh, Mr So-and-So used to do this and that.' Anthony presented me with a sheaf of maps and showed me how to fold them to fit into the map case and the pocket on the front of the right trouser leg. For weeks, I was inundated with maps. We seemed to need several a day and, although the Intelligence Officer was only too willing to hand them out, he utterly refused to accept

*Plaque erected by villagers commemorating the liberation of
St Charles de Percy by the Irish Guards*

old ones back.

Sleeping in a slit trench with a steel helmet as pillow is far from comfortable, but you get used to it and, if you are tired enough, discomfort is less noticeable. Next morning, I took stock. I had twenty-eight men in my platoon, all tested in battle, whereas I was a complete novice, although I knew what to do in theory. Sergeant Wheater, the platoon sergeant, seemed competent and friendly. Even so, it was important not to allow oneself to be borne along on the shoulders of an NCO. The Company Quartermaster Sergeant issued me with a Sten gun but, for the time being, no magazines were available. The binoculars that had been round Thomas Stafford-King-Harmon's neck when he was killed were passed on undamaged to me.

Late in the morning, we were ordered to move closer to the front where desultory crashes and bangs occurred in the distance. Marching through the usual dust, we passed a burnt-out Sherman tank with blackened debris round it. Nearby was a Bren gun with all its wooden parts charred off; fused to the remains of the butt were two hands and wrists, no more. German equipment lay scattered around. We trudged on through a village towards Estry, taking up a position round a farm and dug in. At about half past three next morning, I heard the whistle of approaching shells. A salvo of eight landed about fifteen yards away, in the middle of my platoon area.

As I raised a cautious head from my slit trench to survey the damage, Watts the sentry came running through the darkness, shaken and anxious. 'Oh, my God, Mr Wilson. It's Ferguson. He's had a direct hit.' I hurried over. The platoon area was absolutely silent. A foul smell of cordite and burnt flesh hung in the air. On the crumpled remains of his slit trench was the body of Ferguson, with most of his head missing. Thin spirals of smoke curled up from beneath him. The second sentry came up with his face cut. I sent him off to Company HQ, from where he returned later minus a splinter. Before daylight, Sergeant Wheater and I buried the body deeper.

The other shells had luckily landed between slit trenches. It was pure chance that this harassing fire had landed amongst us, providentially without causing more damage.

To be on the safe side, I spread out the platoon even more in the morning after a visit from Company Sergeant Major Larking who took one look at the remains of Ferguson's trench and said, 'You shouldn't have let him get away with that, sir. His trench was far too shallow. He might be alive now if he'd dug down another couple of feet. Make them dig good deep trenches and stay alive.'

Excellent advice, but trying on the guardsman who digs a deep hole, roofs it and lines it with hay, only to have to move and dig another hole because his platoon commander thinks there is a gap in his defences. Then the company commander may feel one platoon is rather on its own, so he withdraws it slightly and the digging restarts. Finally, the battalion commander may, for instance, want his forward company reinforced on the flank, so he sends up one of the reserve companies, and the spade is pressed into use again. But the process is unavoidable if the maximum effort is to be brought to bear, and this also means doing one's best to avoid losing men unnecessarily. Dig or die became a catchcry.

Chapter 6

Learning About War

The day passed in sleep, weapon cleaning (one section at a time), and general administration, with men remaining in their slit trenches unless there was a need to emerge. At midday, a guardsman pulled his rifle towards him, gripping it by the barrel and managed to shoot himself through the hand. The company commander agreed with me that it was possibly a self-inflicted wound, a court martial offence if it could be proved. At tea-time, as a guardsman rose from his slit trench to collect his ration, a stray burst of harassing machine-gun fire from possibly a thousand yards away hit him in the leg.

Later in the day, the Company Sergeant Major reappeared, looking for Guardsman Ryan: 'How old are you, Ryan?' he asked.

'Nineteen,' was the reply, as Ryan emerged from his slit trench.

'Oh no you're not. You were sixteen when you enlisted last year, below the minimum age, and you didn't have your parents' permission to leave home either. Your mother's claimed you back now. So pack up your kit and come along.'

With tears in his eyes, the unfortunate Ryan picked up his few possessions from the bottom of his slit trench and, with sympathetic comments from his comrades, trudged off behind the CSM, humiliated to be treated like a schoolboy (which to some extent he still was).

The platoon farewelled him with the usual macabre Mick sense of humour:

'Well now, Paddy, your mother needs you more than the graveyard

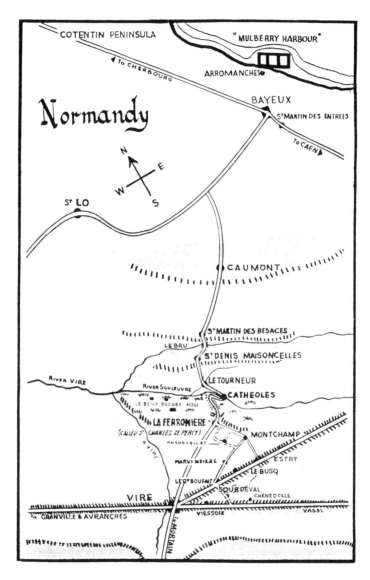

Reproduced by kind permission of Regimental Headquarters, Irish Guards

does.'

'Will you have a Guinness and remember us when you visit our graves?'

'Don't forget you were once a Mick and served where the bullets part the air.'

It was sad that a man who had survived weeks of active service in Normandy should be forced ignominiously to leave his unit and return to peacetime Ireland. But the fact was that his family needed him more, and the general aim was not to send men on active service before their nineteenth birthday. This meant that I was four men down on my first day without ever having been in action.

Odd salvos of shells, in fours or eights, landed nearby. I learnt to recognise the sound of our own artillery firing, the whistle overhead, and the distant explosion. I learnt to listen for the slight thud of a German gun firing, followed by the approaching crescendo of whistle. Further away ahead, a multi-barrelled Nebelwerfer (Moaning Minnie) put down loud crumps, beginning with a winding-up noise, and then a whine sharply descending the scale. These rocket-type mortars produced a deafening explosion but fortunately seldom stayed long in one place, being highly mobile on the backs of vehicles and anxious to move before attracting retaliatory fire.

My administrative education now continued with a study of compo rationing. The system in the 3rd Battalion was that wherever possible the Quartermaster came up with a truck and dumped a few compo boxes with each company. At Company HQ, the Quartermaster Sergeant knew the strength of each platoon and sent out what was required, or more often told the platoon to come and fetch it. (At Company Headquarters, a petrol-operated cooker heated up tins and tea.) In the platoon, all the tins and packets had to be divided up again. Some tins were intended for six men, some for four, and some for two. Problems arose when, for instance, a tin for six was given to a section of five, whilst Platoon Headquarters of six men had only a tin between three.

As I never allowed more than a few men above ground at a time, most of the work of doling out rations was done by Sergeant Wheater and myself. The officer always ate last, having first made sure that his men had received their fair share. More than once, the only tin left over for me had long since lost its label whilst being heated in hot water at Company Headquarters and was unrecognisable in the dark; I can remember my disgust at dining on nothing more than diced carrot.

Breakfast was usually at about 9 am, consisting of biscuits, a piece of bacon or a lump of sausage meat, and some margarine, together with a mug of tea. Lunch could be more biscuits. In the evening, there might be a tin of hot stew and some suet pudding, plus more tea. With usually only cold water available for washing, mess tins remained greasy and unsightly.

The ration also included three sheets of toilet paper. As my servant explained to me when I joined the platoon: 'One up, one down, and one for polishing.' At every platoon position, a latrine trench was dug; full depth at one end and half depth at the other end. You squatted on the half depth platform and threw some loose earth afterwards over the contents in the full depth part.

Every soldier had two identity discs slung on a cord round his neck. Square in shape and made of what looked like plastic, the discs were embossed with the soldier's name, rank, number and religion. One disc was red and the other green. If the soldier was killed, the green disc was left on the body ('to produce green grass') in case of temporary burial and later re-interment in a cemetery of the Commonwealth War Graves Commission; the red disc was collected so that the next-of-kin could be informed.

The days in reserve could be boring. The cycle began at night with stand-to from 2215 hrs to 2300 hrs, when every man stood up in his trench with his weapon ready in case of attack; the minimum of talking and no smoking. From then on, overnight, each section provided a sentry on hourly shifts, except where the platoon was so closed up that a couple of sentries could do for the lot. From 0515 hrs to 0600 hrs was stand-to again. That meant each man got roughly four hours' sleep during the night, bearing in mind his two separate hours of sentry duty. The day, therefore, tended to include some sleeping, letter-writing, weapon cleaning, scrounging, and more sentry duty. My job was to get up at intervals during the night and check that sentries were alert; to wake everyone up at stand-to; to inspect weapons for cleanliness; to censor all letters. This involved crossing out any mention of the names of places or of other units. Some men, particularly married ones, wrote a letter every day. I got used to licking down envelope flaps embellished with SWALK (sealed with a loving kiss) or HTFYITP (hoping this finds you in the pink).

On the third day, I was sent on a reconnaissance patrol to the flank to make contact with whatever troops could be found. The implication was that the Intelligence Officer was far from clear about this. All he knew was that a battalion of the 15th Scottish Division was making an attack on Estry. My job was to find out the position of supporting troops. In the late afternoon of a hot day, I set forth with three guardsmen, to the dismay of Sergeant Wheater who seemed to think we would never meet again. We cautiously made our way through fields and hedges, trying to make sense of the French maps with which we were supplied. Their symbols were different to British ones and there was no legend. A supposed path could turn out to be a contour line.

Finally, I made for the source of sound of a British machine-gun about a mile away. We found a section of the Middlesex Regiment with Vickers machine-guns giving indirect fire on Estry at a range of perhaps a thousand yards. The gunners knew little or nothing of what was happening. Continuing in a circle, we found a group of Gordon Highlanders under the command of a Canadian officer. (At this stage in the war, a shortage of junior officers in the British Army and a surplus in the Canadian Army led to the posting of many Canadian volunteers to British regiments.)

After reporting back to Battalion HQ where the Intelligence Officer (Captain Eric Udal) seemed to know all that I could tell him, I made my way back to my platoon, stopping en route to talk to Anthony Eardley-Wilmot. As we spoke in the roadway, a burst of machine-gun fire from far away passed between us, giving its distinct crack as it parted the air. As a front-line infantryman, you never knew when the end might come. All that training and military skill could be wasted by a chance bullet or shell.

Next day, my platoon was required to relieve one in a more forward company, taking over their positions whilst they went off to some mobile baths in the rear. Our arrival was followed by a furious burst of shelling, one of which landed on the parapet of a trench. The guardsman emerged uninjured but crying, shaking and twitching, looking a mental wreck. I led him off to a nearby barn, sat him down and tried unsuccessfully to calm him. At that moment, CSM Larking appeared on the scene, a veritable giant of regimental efficiency, who seemed to know when I, an inexperienced platoon commander, was in trouble.

He took one look at the guardsman, yelled at him to get up on his feet: 'Pick up your rifle, you useless soldier . . . Stand to attention . . . Slope arms . . . Right turn, left turn . . . As you were . . . Now, in double time, quick march . . . About turn . . . Halt . . . Stand still, you baby.'

And so it went on, with the guardsman transformed at the end of it into a normal soldier.

The CSM turned to me finally as I watched open-mouthed. 'There you are, sir. That's what you should have done.'

'Yes, Sergeant-Major. Thank you, Sergeant-Major,' was all I could say.

Since then, I've lacked confidence (to put it mildly) in the efficacy of the modern trend for counselling. I can just see CSM Larking retorting, 'Counselling? What they need now is a good kick up the arse and be told to get on with it!'

Chapter 7

Sourdeval

On the following day, the battalion was on the move again in daylight, past the burnt-out Sherman and Bren gun, bound for a front-line position. Then we hung about for darkness before embarking in vehicles. Driving without lights, it was necessary to keep in touch with the vehicle ahead, if you could see it through the haze of dust. Once we drove into the Bren carrier ahead, much to its annoyance. As we debussed in a sunken lane, a salvo of shells exploded in the orchard over the hedge. Fifteen yards shorter, and it would have made a mess of a lot of soldiers.

There was a march of about six miles in full kit down a long hill into a valley and up the other side. It turned out to be the furthest we should have to march, stumbling into every pothole there was and choking in the dust. A few aircraft droned over with tracer fire rising towards them. At least it broke the monotony to look up at the blackness of the sky and see red stars climb one above the other, then go out again from the top downwards. There was a distant rattle of small-arms fire with Very lights soaring up now and again, and the sound of shells exploding. We were reaching the real war.

My platoon took over from a platoon of the combined Monmouth and Norfolk Regiments, who were only too pleased to get out. They painted lurid stories of the terrible shelling. A corporal said that the only person who ever got out of his slit trench was the sergeant (they had no officer) who had to do all the work. Apparently a week earlier they had advanced rapidly, only to be bombed by our aircraft which had wrecked all their transport. The Germans counter-attacked and now they were only just holding on.

The change-over was carried out comparatively smoothly as far as the rifle companies were concerned, but it was a different matter for the vehicles, anti-tank guns, and Bren carriers of the Support Company. A double line of traffic in the lane up a steep hill in the dark moved at a snail's pace. Inevitably, there was a fair amount of shouted orders; enough to reach the Germans a few hundred yards away. There was a rush and a roar like a rocket, followed by explosions in the fields either side of the lane. Those were the first 88-mm guns I had heard. Their muzzle velocity was so high that, at short and medium ranges, the whistle of the approaching shell and its explosion were practically simultaneous, thus giving no warning. In this case, they luckily failed to reach their target.

The Monmouths/Norfolks had not roofed over their slits, as a protection against shell fragments and mortar fire. I made the platoon (not that they needed encouragement) roof over the tops with baulks of timber and branches, filling the gaps with hay, and placing a good layer of earth and stones on top, leaving an entrance hole in the middle. The drawback to this protection was that only one person at a time could enter (there can be moments when more than one hurls himself into the nearest slit), and only one person can be in a position to fire. However, we were unlikely to be attacked where we were, and protection against shelling and mortar fire was the first priority.

Next morning I surveyed the platoon area which lay behind the front line in reserve. We did not appear to face any particular direction but lay well protected under a hedge on a reverse slope; we could not even see past the hedge. It seemed a poor choice for a defensive position, but at least it was below the crest of the hill so that shells tended to land further down the valley. On the other hand, our own shells seemed to whistle past just over our heads. Piles of derelict kit lay strewn about; broken rifles, heaps of ammunition, grenades and shattered steel helmets. It was a dismal scene, but not as bad as at Battalion HQ which was sited in an orchard surrounded by burnt-out vehicles and shell holes. In a field nearby were rows of crosses over rough graves, including that of Private Bates of the Norfolks who had been awarded a posthumous VC.

As I walked round the platoon position, a large tree limb damaged by shell fire and loosened by the wind crashed down beside me. If it had killed me, I wondered whether my headstone in a Commonwealth War Graves cemetery would still have carried the inscription 'Killed in action'. Whilst squatting in the latrine trench one morning, a burst of shelling forced me to jump for better cover into the deeper part. Sergeant Wheater, with whom I shared a slit trench, was reluctant to allow me back into our trench. Early one morning, before stand-to, I was woken in the half-light by a shower of earth landing on me. Getting up to investigate, I was in time to find a mole turning round in its hole at the side of the slit trench and making off the way it had come. It had apparently been tunnelling and suddenly found an unexpected abyss in the form of a slit trench.

When watching one of our artillery batteries firing in the distance, I was hailed from the road by a figure with no equipment, wearing a beret and shoes, no gaiters, and his hands in his pockets. This turned out to be a French liaison officer, unworried by the occasional shelling and looking for Battalion HQ. The next interruption was a sudden influx of signallers laying a cable along the road and disturbed by the shelling. How six of us fitted into my slit trench, I cannot imagine. And yet there were long periods when there was no shelling, and all the time the August sun shone hotly down.

On the evening of 10 August, I attended an 'O' (Orders) Group at Company HQ, interrupted by shelling and a dive for cover under a wood pile. We learnt that, at 8.30 am next day, Nos.2 and 4 Companies would carry out an attack either side of a lane (centre line), with tank support from the 1st Battalion Coldstream Guards. Intelligence thought that a breakthrough was possible. All that afternoon, Sherman tanks had rumbled up the road and parked on the other side of the hedge from my platoon, raising clouds of dust and renewed shelling.

Chapter 8

Attack

I passed on the orders to my platoon that night. The other two platoons would advance ahead of mine, with Pod Bourke in front and Company HQ on our right. Next morning there was plenty of shelling from our own artillery. Eight thirty passed and nothing much happened. At nine, we filed off into the road in full kit and made our way up to the start line on the crest of the hill. From there, it looked as if we would have to advance down a forward slope overlooked by a hill opposite.

I spread out the platoon behind our support tank and away we went at the high port with bayonets fixed across a field. Our own artillery was still firing over our heads, but something went wrong and a shell exploded about fifteen yards away on my right. Several then landed between me and the platoon ahead, fortunately without causing injury. Somewhat rattled, we continued on through the next hedge into a field of standing wheat, with a thick hedge about fifty yards away on the right.

A Spandau was firing from somewhere on the right. German shells started to rain down. Men from the platoons ahead had gone to ground. I shouted to them to keep going and moved forward myself crouching. My platoon was now mingled with the forward troops. When mortar bombs began to land round me, I followed the general example and lay flat on my face, followed by my runner and Platoon HQ behind me. A shell burst about five yards away on my right, wounding the man in front of me, the man behind, and the man on my left. I who was nearest escaped unhurt. One of the wounded was Corporal Carroll, a piper whose

The Ever Open Eye

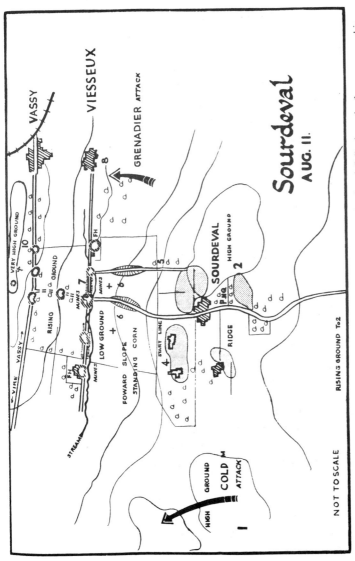

High ground (1), originally held by enemy, overlooked approaches to Sourdeval and O.Ps. brought fire on approaching vehicles. This danger passed after Coldstream attack. The high ground at (10) road and forward slope between (7) and (10) just visible from (4) and (5). (b) equals gentle forward slope in full view of enemy positions located by patrols. Track (6) deep cutting where most casualties occurred, the stream *not* an obstacle.

Reproduced by kind permission of Regimental Headquarters, Irish Guards

operational function was to act as stretcher-bearer. I crawled over to him, and he directed me to a pair of scissors in his pocket. I cut off his sleeve, whereupon a torrent of blood poured out all over me from a wound on his arm near the armpit. Putting a shell dressing on the wound, I sent him back to the Regimental Aid Post.

A figure came bounding past me through the corn. It was Pod Bourke. I shouted to him to keep down as the Spandau was still firing from the right. He muttered something about his platoon being in the wrong place and continued on. At this stage, it was apparent that forward movement had ceased. I felt I could not lie still and do nothing, so continued to crawl forward and shouted to others to do the same.

Shells and mortars still crashed down; men screamed as they were hit. It was obvious that the enemy could clearly observe us, perhaps from the hill opposite. In desperation, I shouted to my two mortar men, who had somehow managed to keep up with me, to put down a couple of rounds of smoke upwind to screen us from view. They did so and immediately a cloudburst of German mortar bombs rained down on them. I later found one of my mortar men dead with his brains splashed over the baseplate. I was conscience-stricken and, although it may have been just the fortune of war, I have always felt responsible for his death.

One or more Spandaus were still firing from the right at anyone above the level of the corn. Fortunately, there was a slight rise in the ground between us and the Spandaus, so we were reasonably safe from them (but not from shells and mortars) if we lay flat in the corn. On the other hand, we could not fire back as there was no field of vision from the ground, nor was it possible to locate where the fire was coming from. Crawling forward, I came to a swathe, perhaps five yards wide, where the corn had been cut, dividing the top and bottom of the field. The slow moving traffic piled up here, with men reluctant to expose themselves to the Spandau.

I reckoned from my own experience that it takes at least three seconds to swing a machine-gun and fire a well-aimed burst, by which time I ought with luck to get across the gap. Twice I gathered myself together ready for the dash and twice nothing happened. My legs refused to act.

My subconscious mind had taken over and left me literally paralysed with fear. The third time I moved like a rocket in a dive to the other side, hitting the ground so hard that I felt quite dazed. A burst of Spandau fire passed harmlessly overhead, as I crawled rapidly away. My example led another guardsman to follow me across the gap.

We were now more than half-way down the field, some 300 yards from the start line. My platoon was scattered; the advance had ceased; and the initiative lay with the Germans. Our supporting tanks were unable to help. One had been knocked out at the start; a second had tipped over on its side in a sunken lane on the right; the third was firing its Browning from the middle of the cornfield in front, whilst the fourth was moving up and down the lane that formed the centre line. Being on a forward slope, neither of the two tanks still in action could depress its guns enough to search the ground in front. Consequently they were no help. The tank in the corn was soon hit by an 88, causing the crew to bale out and depart.

I kept crawling to my left and with other men entered the centre-line lane, hoping that its thick banks and hedges would offer some protection from the Spandaus, mortars, and 88. I applied dressings on a couple more wounded men and stopped beside a wireless operator with an 18 set strapped on his back. At that moment, a number of guardsmen burst through the hedge on the left where No. 4 Company was advancing, followed by Major Desmond Reid, their company commander. The Spandau opened up and caught him in the leg in mid air almost over my head where I lay in the lane. As he landed, his leg doubled up and he was assisted off the scene by a couple of guardsmen. The new arrivals said that Lieutenant Lord Edward Fitzmaurice lay dead on the other side of the hedge. That, apparently, left me as the sole officer with the remnants of two companies. I radioed Battalion HQ for instructions and was told to dig in and consolidate.

Alongside me was Piercey, a more elderly guardsman and company clerk. How he got involved in the battle, I don't know, but he was cheerful and got on with trying to dig a slit trench in the pavé lane with the aid of an entrenching tool. We had all of us long since discarded our spades which were carried into battle under the belt with the blade across the chest, where it was too inconvenient for crawling. The entrenching tool, on the other hand, was carried in a webbing holder on the belt.

Between us, Piercey and I dug down about six inches. Kneeling there, I was looking down the lane when there was an explosion in front of me. I saw the blinding orange flame of the explosion which rocked me backwards, and felt a short stab in my right chest. A mortar bomb had burst only feet away and left me living. Piercey beside me was untouched, except for a few bits through his equipment and a chunk in the heel of his boot. I received a small fragment in the chest (it is still there), and I later removed tiny pieces from my leg and knee. It was my second lucky escape of the day.

All the time the sun shone brightly, and I was tortured with thirst. A dead guardsman lay face down in front of me; on the other side of the lane a Monmouth lad, obviously dead for some time, lay on his back. His face and hands were green and covered in flies. The smell was penetrating.

The sunken lane near Sourdeval, which formed the centre line of the disastrous attack, 11 August 1944

The Ever Open Eye

The tank in the lane still rumbled up and down ahead of us beyond where our group of guardsmen was holed up. Once it reversed straight for Piercey and myself, partially over the dead guardsman ahead. We yelled and managed to stop it, whereupon it reversed up the lane and departed, much to our relief as it attracted fire from the 88. A shell hit the hedge about ten yards away, wounding a guardsman in the head. When Piercey reached him, he was on his face choking in a pool of his own blood.

A faint plopping noise came from the middle of the cornfield on the right. There was nothing to be seen at first but gradually a small column of smoke rose to meet the sun. There was a crackling of fire amongst the dry stalks of the corn, caused presumably by the phosphorous grenades that the Germans were throwing. It looked as if, fearful of our creeping up on them through the corn, they had decided to burn it notwithstanding any wounded still lying there. But the fire was fairly limited and no danger to ourselves in the lane.

I was still digging in the lane when a German must have loosed a

The hedges have gone from the sunken lane fifty years later

burst of automatic fire from further down the lane. The first I knew was when a burst kicked up the dust between my arm and my body, missing me by inches. I flung myself flat and feared the worst. But nothing more happened, except for a few bursts overhead and they tailed off. My third lucky escape that day.

I pondered what to do. If I charged down the lane firing my Sten gun, I might have thirty yards to go to reach an unlocated enemy, with no covering fire from the flank. Even if I knew the target, it was quite far to hurl a grenade and follow up on foot. In the end, I did nothing. On reflection over the years, this may have been a mistake. I should have led a charge with maximum fire power, although it might have proved costly. In war, it sometimes pays not to do too much thinking but to move resolutely and speedily. In the event here, it did not matter, as the Germans withdrew that night anyway. But a successful action at the end might have done something to redress the balance of the failed IG attack.

We had now been four hours in this dismal advance which had quite obviously ground to a halt. As there was no point in our continuing to suffer casualties by crouching in the lane, I wirelessed to Battalion HQ and, receiving permission to withdraw, organised the removal of the wounded from the lane and the withdrawal of the unwounded in bounds to make sure we were not shot up from behind. Meanwhile I set up a Bren gun in the hedge and fired at likely spots on the other side of the field, moving my position rapidly in case of being spotted.

I handed over the gun to a guardsman whilst I tried to locate with my binoculars. Thinking I could see something, I gave him a fire order. He raised the butt to his shoulder but unfortunately pushed the gun forward through the hedge, whereupon a burst of bullets from the flank caught him across the back. I tore off his tunic and applied a dressing to three jagged rips across his back over his shoulder blade, just missing his spine.

Thereafter, I kept the gun to myself, firing at random along the opposite hedge, until the gun jammed. Under the critical gaze of a Bren gunner, I ran through the usual drill for clearing stoppages and got going again. Time to withdraw. This meant crawling for what felt like a hundred yards on hands and knees over the stones and flints of the pavé lane, as the hedges higher up were low and the systematic shelling by the 88s had blown gaps in them.

At the top, I met more survivors who had been further over to the right. William Harvey-Kelly beamed in surprise to see me still alive. He was organising a scratch force sited just in front of the original start line, to repel any German counter-attack. He told me Pod Bourke had been killed, as had Anthony Eardley-Wilmot and the Company Sergeant Major. We lay in position for some time, but as there was no sign of German movement, I was permitted to leave for the Regimental Aid Post. My chest was now beginning to be painful. The muscles on the right were so stiff that I could hardly move my arm, aggravated by the weight of my equipment.

Outside the RAP was a pile of discarded and often bloodstained tunics, boots, equipment, weapons, helmets, and other items. Alongside was a shattered stretcher, its canvas full of holes. As the stream of casualties had fallen off, I felt justified in presenting my little hole for inspection. It turned out to be quite small, although it had bled a lot. The splinter had passed through a strap of my equipment, tunic, braces and shirt. Fortified with a dressing and a cup of tea, I tried to quieten a guardsman sitting nearby moaning and shaking uncontrollably from shell-shock. Again unsuccessful, but this time there was no company sergeant major to take over.

As I left, a surprised guardsman drew attention to the tin mug hanging from a strap on the small pack on my back. It was so riddled with holes as to be little more than a handle. The rolled gas cape on the back of my belt was also torn to shreds. This must have happened on the first of my lucky escapes when a shell burst beside me as I lay flat. Since then, I've tried to stay slim in case the same should happen again.

The RAP told me that twenty-eight men and three officers had been killed and sixty-six wounded in this unsuccessful attack. From first to last of this disastrous day, I never saw a German, nor did many of the other guardsmen involved.

Reporting to Battalion HQ, I found Lieutenant-Colonel Joe washing his hair in a green canvas bucket. He was very considerate on being told what I knew of the battle and offered me tea which I gratefully drank. The Intelligence Officer, Captain Eric Udal, ran through the story with me. Then, delayed reaction set in and I started to shiver violently. The Regimental History puts me down as collapsing. This is rubbish. I was very much in charge of myself but in the grip of temporary reaction to the horrors of my first day in action.

Going forward again, I found that, as a leading light of a battle school in England, Lieutenant Edward Rawlence, the Motor Transport Officer, had been put in charge of reorganisation in case of a German counter-attack. We sat about tired and dispirited whilst our artillery put down a smoke screen to allow survivors to withdraw; three emerged. Just before dark, we withdrew to our former company positions, leaving a screen of soldiers from another unit to hold the line. The CO gathered the survivors and explained that the attack had failed because it lacked enough support, in particular of artillery (only one battery of guns made available) and had taken place down a forward slope overlooked ahead and on the left by rising ground on which were sited German artillery and observation posts. The odds were so stacked against us that there was really little hope of success. It was many years later before I discovered that the Monmouth and Norfolk battalion whom we had relieved had shortly before carried out a similar attack with equally disastrous results. There was no reason to suppose that the Irish Guards would fare any better. In short, the attack was probably doomed before it started.

My original platoon now numbered only four men; others were also depleted. Nos.2 and 4 Companies were, therefore, amalgamated and I finished up with a strong platoon again. Luckily, several officers had been LOB (left out of battle; a standard practice before action where casualties were likely) and they now appeared on the scene. Captain Alec Hendry took over No.2 Company. The second in command of the Brigade, a Colonel, came round with the Commanding Officer to talk to survivors. Seeing my gloomy face, the Colonel clapped me on the back (on my aching shoulder), told me I was perfectly all right, and should be ready to fight again. Company Sergeant Major Larking might have approved of this approach, but it left me unconvinced.

Chapter 9

The Aftermath of Battle

My hands and arms were filthy with a thick coating of dried blood and dust. My wrist-watch was so red under the glass that I could scarcely read the dial. There was no chance of washing and little energy to do so. I slept like a log, failing to check sentries overnight. In the morning, summoned to Battalion HQ, I was ordered to lead a reconnaissance patrol over the battlefield to check whether the Germans had retired during the night. There were reports that they had gone.

(Later I discovered that Lieutenant Andrew Philp, Coldstream Guards, who had been at Pirbright and the OCTU with me, was probably the source of this intelligence. On patrol that night, on the right of the IG, he had heard vehicles returning all night from the German front.)

I took two guardsmen. We passed through the forward company (Scots Guards temporarily forming part of the 3rd Battalion Irish Guards) and slunk down the centre-line lane. The sun was high in the sky and the dead were smelling badly. When we reached the place where I had sheltered in a slit on the previous day, the stench was terrible. The Monmouth lad had turned black and was beginning to decompose.

Scanning the countryside with binoculars, I could see no sign of the enemy. Taking a towel from a discarded small pack, I poked it through the hedge on the end of a rifle and bayonet and waved it about. No reaction. I threw smoke grenades into the fields on either side of the lane. I fired a few shots at likely places and shifted position quickly. Satisfied that there were no Germans about, we returned up the lane and went off to the right and there found Pod Bourke kneeling dead behind a hedge with his head on his chest and a little dried blood on his neck and side. A shell splinter must have hit him.

The CO and IO seemed doubtful when I reported no sign of Germans. Walking back, I met some Coldstream tanks and gave their troop commander a Coldstream cap star I found in the lane when returning from patrol. At Company HQ, Alec Hendry told me to go for a couple of days to B Echelon (administrative tail of the battalion). Edward Rawlence drove me there past green fields to a farm with the battalion's vehicles parked against hedges under camouflage nets. I located my platoon truck, extracted my valise and slept for two nights on my camp bed.

This was not altogether as comfortable as it might have been. As new, the regular Army camp bed of those days stood about eighteen inches off the ground. With use, the canvas stretched and the height decreased until you found yourself sleeping with the canvas pressing against the wooden slats beneath. Eventually, it became more comfortable to sleep on the ground. I spent my time washing in the cold local stream, tidying things up, and visiting Captain Thynne, the Medical Officer. He changed the dressing on my chest and decided to leave the fragment where it was. He reckoned it might do more damage to try and extract it than to let it be. I met John Luxembourg, now posted as Liaison Officer and interpreter at Brigade HQ.

At the end of two days, I rejoined the battalion which had been withdrawn and shifted to the flank. My platoon was up to strength, so we spent ten days out of the line doing drill in the mornings, PT in the afternoons, and between times checking weapons and equipment. Compo rations were supplemented by whatever the men could scrounge: potatoes, eggs, milk. A NAAFI ration appeared with cigarettes, tobacco, writing paper, and even beer.

The summer sun of mid August shone hotly, allowing men to wear nothing but PT shorts and boots. Many of them looked like tanned bathing instructors. Sergeant Sullivan, one of my section commanders and a good athlete, told me he had just been offered a job at a beach rest camp. But the poor man never had a chance to take up the offer before we moved again. Since we seemed to be beyond average shelling range, most men slept above ground, but I played safe and still slept in a slit trench.

The four company officers ate their compo rations together. With Alec Hendry as company commander, the platoon commanders were John Stanley-Clarke, William Harvey-Kelly and myself. We were joined by Bobby Taylor who had served briefly in North Africa and Italy. Because he spoke better French than the rest of us, he was made to scour the countryside for eggs, corn on the cob, wine and other delicacies. I also carried out the unhappy task of writing to the next-of-kin of the members of my platoon killed at Sourdeval. In one case, something must have gone wrong with the system, because a parent wrote back to enquire what was wrong with his son and why I had sent a letter of condolence. Obviously, my letter had reached him before the dreaded telegram from the War Office with the news of his son's death.

Alec and I revisited the scene of the disastrous attack of 11 August at Sourdeval. Burial parties had provided temporary graves and crosses in the positions where the dead had fallen, so that it was possible to work out roughly what had happened. I found where my entire forward section under Sergeant Cooke had been wiped out in the middle of the cornfield where it had been burnt. I tried to push down a hand that stuck out from one of the graves, only to find that it fell apart into a heaving, wriggling mass of maggots. The German positions had been cunningly concealed and protected from shelling by a sunken lane. Our attack in daylight had followed the most obvious route with no cover. If our tanks had reached the road at the bottom of the valley, they might have been able to break the crust of the German line which did not seem to be in depth. One tank, a Firefly with a 17-pounder gun, had tried but took the hedge and sunken road diagonally, and fell over on its side.

Over on the right was a farm which turned out to contain a winery with its own electric light plant and huge vats now wrecked by shell fire. The house was empty but in a dreadful mess. It looked as if the Germans had ransacked the place, piling up breakable objects and soft furnishings over which cider, vinegar and other liquids had been poured. But the cellar was stocked with bottles of red and white wine, so I took the liberty of filling a couple of sacks with bottles.

Next day, I mentioned this to Lieutenant Johnny Gough of the Bren Carrier platoon (we had been together at Pirbright and the OCTU). We drove back to the farm in a captured German Volkswagen. This was a tiny amphibious run-about, with a propeller and engine at the back, and the manoeuvrability of a dodg'em car. Being very light, it was unstable over rough ground and much of the way had been churned up by tracked vehicles.

At one spot where there was a pool of water at the bottom of a slope, we had no option but to drive through it. The hedges either side prevented our making a detour. In the middle of the muddy pool, we hit a rut and the vehicle turned on its side; my side. I was forced to get into the water and push the vehicle to the other end of the pool, gloomily contemplating the return journey over the same route.

At the farm, we loaded a sackful of bottles into the Volkswagen and were filling a second sack in the cellar when we heard a noise outside. To our horror, it proved to be the owner.

Leaving Johnny to empty the bottles from the sack as fast as he could, I dashed outside and tried desperately to engage the owner in lengthy conversation so as to give Johnny time to finish unloading. Unfortunately, in his haste, he knocked bottles together. The owner heard, at once realised what was going on, and hurried indoors, catching us red-handed. We apologised profusely and bought one bottle for 100 francs (ten shillings at the then rate), which was an inflated price intended to atone for an embarrassing situation. We hurried off, taking care that the other two dozen bottles already in the Volkswagen did not betray themselves by clanging together.

It was, of course, improper to loot in this manner, bearing in mind that the farmer had little enough to come back to, with his farmhouse damaged, its contents vandalised, and his stock of animals diminished. Dead cows lay everywhere, with swollen bellies and their feet straight up in the air. Having lived beside both, it seemed to me that dead cows smelt worse than dead men. Pouring petrol over a dead cow and lighting it did little more than singe its hide.

Pigs appeared to suffer from shell-shock more than other farm animals. Several times I met unfortunate pigs running round in circles, grunting and squealing and bumping into objects, butting gates and fences with their heads. Poultry wandered round farms looking lost and bewildered. Tame rabbits watched from all corners as you entered a farmyard. Turning a corner, there would be a lazy scamper under a box or a shy pair of ears peering round a barrel.

Several guardsmen from the country milked cows with swollen udders, although not all cows welcomed this attention. There would occasionally be an unseemly scuffle with a swearing guardsman and no milk. The surviving cows lumbered cautiously into forbidden fields of corn or the vegetable garden where they caused havoc.

Many German positions could be located by the foul smell from them, the result partly of poor latrine discipline and partly rotting food: often cheese and sausage meat.

My platoon never seemed to stop eating. Whenever I made my way round checking on sentries and getting to know this new lot of guardsmen, there were little fires everywhere and pots of stew simmering. The utensils came from a nearby farm whose owner had only just come back into residence. Le patron's daughter took a poor view of this 'borrowing' and made periodic rounds of the area to recover what she could. This caused much fun. As she came through the gate into the field, there would be cries of 'Watch your kit, boys'. Immediately, pots and pans would be stuffed into the bottoms of slit trenches; boxes hidden under blankets, with everyone sitting tight. The girl would poke around and remove what she could, accompanied by good-natured cries of woe from the guardsmen. Even I was not exempt. The chair that I used to 'borrow' was taken away, to the amusement of the platoon. It was all cheerful badinage, with the girl speaking not a word of English and the guardsmen none of French. I was always the interpreter.

Chapter 10

Filling in Time

It was now the latter part of August. The weather broke and it frequently poured with rain. I tried sleeping under a piece of green canvas otherwise used to envelop my kit in the platoon truck, but it proved to be far from waterproof. On the other hand, my camp bed was waterproof and therefore held the water, meaning that I lay in wetness under a sagging, dripping canvas.

The guardsmen built themselves little bivouacs and kept reasonably dry, except for two whom I found one morning half-submerged. They looked so miserable that I hunted round the farmhouse for a shed, where they installed themselves beside a couple of pigs. My runner, Shackleton, adept at looking after himself, had scrounged the folding roof of a carriage under which he lived in comfort. A few days later, I was approached by two irate Normans demanding the return of their property which was, of course, the folding hood. I promised to arrange this and told Shackleton so. Next day he still had the hood. On my asking why, he assured me airily that he had fixed things up with the farmer. I had my doubts but let the matter stand.

With others of my platoon, I took the opportunity of practising marksmanship by firing a Bren and Sten from the hip at the run. At thirty yards, in a steady jog trot, we all did fairly well aiming at a tin can. I even became reasonably proficient firing my revolver with either hand. The platoon officer and the three lance-sergeants in charge of sections were each armed with a Sten gun.

The remainder of the platoon carried rifles: the Short Magazine Lee Enfield (SMLE) Mark 3 which was single-shot and accurate up to 300 yards when the bayonet was fixed. It had an aperture backsight which could be flipped over to a different size of hole, depending on whether the target was up to 300 yards away or further. You aimed by aligning the foresight in the centre of the aperture and on the target. The kick and the noise of the explosion when firing the rifle could be disconcerting at first, and required a firm grip of the rifle to ensure accuracy, plus plenty of practice with live ammunition.

This idle life ended. We struck camp, handed back 'borrowed' items, cleared the area, and embussed in the late afternoon to catch up with the battlefront which was now rapidly moving north towards the Seine. The battle of the Falaise Gap had finished and it was now a matter of racing ahead in our proper role of lorried infantry in an armoured division. The convoy moved at a prescribed slow pace, at so many vehicles to the mile (VTM).

At first, we passed through battlefields with brewed-up tanks, torn hedges, and churned up fields. Because of the damage their tracks caused to roads, our tanks now tended to travel across country along taped tracks that led straight through hedges. For us in troop carrying vehicles, it was a slow progress until we came to the fine main road between Vire and Aunay-sur-Odon, allowing us to move faster for once. Aunay was a mess, having suffered a heavy bombing raid by the RAF. It now consisted of nothing but rubble with not a whole house standing. Bulldozers had cleared a road through, between heaps of bricks and debris.

Beyond Condé-sur-Noireau, still well behind the battlefront, we debussed in yet another orchard, where we dug in and passed the time peacefully. There was even a Brigade boxing tournament between the Irish Guards and Welsh Guards. The Divisional Commander, Major General Adair, turned up; roads and lanes were choked with vehicles; and spectators cheered themselves hoarse. The contest ended in a draw, but the verdict was given to the Welsh Guards on the grounds of their superior aggressiveness. This provoked a howl of fury from the Micks and a derisive cheer from the Taffs. The world may have wondered why, in the midst of a war, soldiers on the same side should fight each other instead of the enemy. But this was the way of the Army, to allow men to let off steam and take their minds off the war.

On 26 August with the aid of the local Curé and the Quartermaster, Battalion HQ organised a party for local French children. Thirty children were invited; a hundred and ten appeared, all hungry and determined to eat us out of house and home. Entertainment afterwards was provided by the pipers in their corbeens and saffron kilts, and also by the Battalion's despatch riders doing some trick riding on their motor cycles, fortunately with no casualties. The children ran races and played games, distension proving no handicap. The Curé followed with a splendid speech of thanks which few of us understood.

This period of rest provided the opportunity to meet other officers. Arriving as a reinforcement and then restricted to my own platoon area, I had never seen half the officers in the battalion; David Stevenson of the Welsh Guards, who had been at school with me and whom I had last seen in Aldershot and Bayeux, paid a visit. He gave me news of several other people and made the world seem wider than a platoon in some orchard.

I used to walk a lot, watching out for mines and booby-traps, although the area had not been the scene of any battles. There were lots of mushrooms, though, which I collected and cooked. Walking down a lane one day with a bulging handkerchief, I was surprised to meet a Chinese dressed in the usual Norman garb for men, of blue overalls, black beret, and wooden sabots. He beamed, pointed at my bundle, and said 'Mushroom?' This appeared to be the extent of his English. After that, I often met Chinese in the district; old and young, all speaking French. The women dressed after the fashion of Norman women in a long-sleeved black dress and black stockings.

Chapter 11

Advance of the Guards Armoured Division

On 28 August the advance of the Guards Armoured Division began. Hitherto, in Normandy, we had operated separately as armour and infantry. Now we were to work together, as originally intended. Starting at 1 am, we drove all night through pouring rain which continued on the following day. The armour travelled somewhere behind us on transporters, whilst we, the infantry, sat in TCVs doing our best to catch up the battle which lay some distance ahead. Donovan, my RASC driver, with flashing white teeth, never seemed to tire.

By the second day, I gave up trying to follow where we were on the map, as I could not stay awake and, in any case, could not see anything outside through the rain. We simply followed the vehicle in front, through Argentan, Laigle, and Gisors.

At night, we harboured in a field. But the daytime driving was not unbroken movement. At first, we stopped every half-mile in interminable delays, whereupon the men would jump out to stretch their legs. A shout from me or the sentry with the Bren and everyone hurried on board again as we set off once more. If a vehicle in front had engine trouble or went off the road, the short delay in driving round it was multiplied down the column until the tail might be held up for an hour or so. The first two nights were so wet and miserable that we were issued with a rum ration. To my surprise, several guardsmen refused it; it was left to me to drink their share instead.

Beyond Evreux, the country ceased to be Norman bocage but became undulating with large fields and small hedges. We reached the Seine at Vernon, crossed on a pontoon bridge that quivered alarmingly under the vehicle, and met the first truckloads of German prisoners. Up the long slope on the other side of the river, we passed the scene of a battle shortly before, with small packs, equipment and broken weapons scattered about. We scraped gingerly past a burnt-out Tiger tank (German), with its body hidden behind a bend and its gun pointing down the road.

On the morning of 30 August we passed through Beauvais, liberated only hours beforehand; in one end and out the other so quickly that no memory of the place remains with me. The route now approached the battlefields of World War I. The countryside was very bare with long rolling hills giving a view of a mile or two. Looking back from the crest of a hill, the column of vehicles nose-to-tail stretched unendingly in a stream of dust and olive brown. I was told that, closed up, the Division stretched some forty miles down the single road and that, if the normal VTM had been followed, the column might have been 150 miles long. The rate of advance increased and quite often we bowled down the road at a really fast pace. We had no idea what was happening in front, but it was obvious that there was little or no German opposition.

Occasionally, we passed a line of German horse-drawn wagons that had been shot up by the RAF or armoured cars of the Household Cavalry at the head of the GAD. Much of the German transport was horse-drawn and therefore slow-moving in their current withdrawal. Flaming and smoking wagons by the wayside became commonplace, with dead horses, too. At first, I could not understand how shells or bullets could inflict such strange injuries on the horses. The skin and flesh would be completely gone, leaving the bones standing out pink and shining. Further forward, the answer was apparent, when we passed an eager group of women wielding long knives on a newly shot horse. Rationing and shortage of food had caused the French population to suffer, and this free horse flesh was a delicacy long denied them.

The local population here was not so reserved as the Normans. They waved and shouted, hung out flags and generally showed every sign of welcome as we passed. It gradually became commonplace to see what appeared to be every single inhabitant of a village or group of houses standing or sitting in chairs at the wayside, cheering us on and making a day of it in their new-found liberty from curfew and German occupation.

The convoy now stopped only with engine trouble or when the TCV in front stopped. This meant that we ignored German stragglers in the fields. Most had no firearms and looked only for someone to protect them from the FFI, the French underground army which now came out in force with captured German weapons.

At one stop, there was a flurry of shots in a wood to one side and a group of Germans raced towards our vehicles, led by an officer who leapt into the TCV amongst the astonished guardsmen and attempted to hide under a seat, imploring protection from the French who were murdering his men. As we were in no position to take prisoners, we handed him over to the FFI, all wearing on their sleeves a white armlet with the four emblems of a pack of cards: spade, heart, club and diamond. Young and old men, boys and girls, strode vigorously round carrying German rifles over their shoulders and stick grenades in their belts, trying to find a belligerent German. In practice, almost all the Germans still in the area would have been lines of communication troops, probably far from anxious to carry on the war single-handed.

Up to now, we had had no battle at all. Every day was just an uncomfortable ride in the TCV, map reading, boredom, irregular meals and cheering people. I tried to keep the men interested as far as possible with details of the route and its historical associations. In this World War I zone, we saw Vimy Ridge in the distance and at one stage halted beside the first Commonwealth War Graves Commission cemetery that I had ever seen. Filled with Australian graves from World War I, the crosses stretched row after row. Beyond the Somme, we passed more and more cemeteries, all beautifully cared for despite the war. At the Australian cemetery sat a French lad with a drawing board on which he sketched freehand in pencil the various armoured cars, tanks, vehicles and soldiers that had passed by ahead of us. He was a fine artist.

We crossed the Somme just south of Amiens and wound up the other side of the valley. In one village, a veteran with a wooden leg and an ancient bugle gave us a rendering of various British Army bugle calls. We threw him cigarettes. As we moved off, he brought the house down with 'Come to the cookhouse door, boys'. That afternoon we found two temporary graves of Grenadiers, bringing home that there was a shooting war up front. Towards evening the country levelled out and we entered the first captured aerodrome with shattered German aircraft but intact buildings. An armoured car full of RAF Regiment was already taking possession.

That evening, 1 September, we entered Arras, our first big town which had been captured with little or no opposition. I was ordered to take my platoon out in the TCV to the St Pol road and form a roadblock there. It was half-dark, the map did not coincide with what was on the ground and I was rapidly losing patience in the face of an enthusiastic crowd of local well-wishers who were useless in guiding me to the St Pol road. Exasperated, I chose what I thought was the right place and set out the platoon. It turned out eventually to be the right place. The crowds pressed in and would not go away. I just hoped there would be no German attack and gave strict orders to the platoon that no one should leave the platoon area.

I myself sought to discover Company HQ and William Harvey-Kelly's platoon which was supposed to be on my right. This was easier said than done. Shots were still being fired in the distance, but were probably more in the nature of *joie de vie* than actual warfare. I crept along in the dark, cautiously avoiding civilians but did not escape the attentions of an old man who button-holed me in the highest spirits. He was obviously drunk and mad with joy at liberation. Grabbing me by the arm, he led me to a doorway where he insisted on my meeting the local Resistance group.

The doorway led into a low dive crammed with Resisters in various stages of intoxication. They greeted me with howls of glee and pressed me to accept little glasses of cognac. It must have been fairly well watered, as it had no effect on me. I was cheered, clapped, questioned and pestered for souvenirs. They nearly tore the stars off my shoulders. I eventually kept souveniring at bay by offering a 36 grenade, although I had no intention of letting go of it. They sang 'Tipperary' in English (which they did not otherwise speak) for the first two lines and then relapsed into dah-dee-dah. Throughout this part of France, 'Tipperary' was often sung to us at various stops.

Having been thoroughly pawed over, I was shown into a back room where *le patron* introduced me to his inner circle. Each voiced his opinion that Hitler was kaput and the war was just about over. 'A fortnight more, perhaps?' with a Gallic shrug of the shoulders.

In vain, I protested that the war might be over for them but not for us. At this stage I was told I must meet a good friend, a German. This left me uncertain what to do, but it was too late to dither. An unshaven fair-haired lad in civilian clothes, of the same age as myself (twenty), was presented. He put out his hand, and the room went quiet whilst all watched to see my reaction. In a split second, I reckoned that, if the Resistance here accepted this German deserter when they were hellbent elsewhere on murdering stragglers, then it would not do for me to refuse to shake his hand. So I shook it, and the room echoed to cheers. We had a drink together to the downfall of the Reich.

It suddenly struck me that I had been over half an hour away from my platoon. Offering my apologies and bowing to all (Sten gun in one hand), I tried to squirm my way out. This was looked at askance. What was I, a perfectly healthy young man, doing by myself on such a momentous night? *Le Patron* popped through bead curtains and produced Nina who linked arms with me. It appeared that she was mine for the evening and, please, would I send her back when I had finished? We plunged into the crowd where I contrived to lose her and then ran rapidly back to my platoon. Sergeant Ennis, the platoon sergeant, sniffed audibly at my breath when I spoke to him. It was with a certain smugness that I intercepted two guardsmen trying to wander off into the town. It was unlikely that they would escape trouble.

Throughout the night, we were kept awake by drunken revellers regaling us with heartfelt thanks for liberation. About 3 am, it poured with rain and my slit trench, sited in the dark amidst the tins and bottles of the local rubbish dump, began to fill with water. I walked back to the parking place, woke up Donovan and made him bring the TCV forward so that we could all get in (except for the sentries who had to remain in the trenches). It then stopped raining.

The morning dawned bright and cheerful, with the war seemingly far away; there was even a bird singing. During the night, the town had appeared full of drunks; the day brought a flood of respectability. Those who had prudently barricaded themselves, their families and their property during the night now emerged to greet us. With the platoon, I gave up all pretence of control and just implored everyone not to go too far away. I sat down to a pleasant breakfast in a well-swept garage, cleaned my weapons (Sten and .38 Smith & Wesson revolver) before an admiring crowd, and was invited into a large house where I was able to shave and wash in a real bathroom.

As the morning drew on, large numbers of people in smart clothes strolled gaily down the road. The crowds were making their way to La Grande Place to see the public humiliation of the women collaborators. Local girls who had consorted with German soldiers were due to have their heads shaved. Several of these girls appeared later in public, seemingly unabashed, with their heads covered in turbans and scarves of the red, white and blue in the French flag.

The enthusiasm of the local population was tremendous. They beamed all over whenever they saw a British soldier, handkerchiefs fluttered everywhere in recognition, and hands were shaken in a never-ending stream. In the background was a lyrical chorus of '*Vive L'Angleterre* . . . Hullo Tommee . . . Ceegarette . . . Hurrah.'

The FFI apparently commandeered any civilian vehicle that would move (most had been stationary without fuel for the whole period of German occupation). Fuel now came from captured German stocks or the British Army. Weapons were largely seized from surrendering Germans. These old vehicles roared down the roads, tooting loudly, surrounded with clinging figures waving rifles and eager for some sort of action as they went off into the blue chasing Germans. This was their moment of revenge after four years of enemy occupation. They organised patrols round the district and were a useful source of information. But the strain was often too much for vehicles suffering from years of neglect.

Company Headquarters had never less than a couple of broken-down vehicles outside it, awaiting attention from the harassed MT Sergeant.

On my way to Company HQ, I met a young French girl perhaps twelve years old. Filled with the euphoria of liberation, she gazed brightly up at me, and exclaimed '*Mon brave soldat. Embrasse-moi. Je veux t'embrasser.*' I bent down, put an arm round her (the other holding my Sten), and gave her a chaste salute on the cheek. At that moment, my servant and another guardsman came round the corner. On seeing this touching scene, they burst out laughing. 'Oh, Mr Wilson, sir. Is it cradle snatching you are? Would you like us to find you a bigger girl?'

At midday, we said goodbye to our hosts, as it were, cleared up the platoon area, and made our way to Company HQ. Despite my orders, one guardsman was drunk and propped up by his comrades. He was normally a quiet fellow who presumably had been led astray by well-meaning French people unaware that many British of those days were unaccustomed to wine and did not know when they had had enough. But it did not improve my temper. At least he had the grace to be very ashamed afterwards.

The day's trip in TCVs took us to Douai. En route, we passed the smoking wreckage of yet more German transport shot up by the leading troops (Household Cavalry and Coldstream Guards). The story was that the FFI had thoughtfully altered the signposts so that the retreating Germans, instead of going northwards, had mistakenly gone southwards, to meet the GAD head-on. The first sight in Douai was of a group of Coldstream collecting German dead. I recognised Guardsman Phillips, servant of David Boyle who had served in the OCTU at Aldershot with me. The next time I met Phillips was in Queen Mary's Hospital, Roehampton, where he was recovering from the loss of an arm at Beeringen on the Albert Canal in Belgium.

We passed a quiet uneventful night in Douai, in an area some distance beyond the actual town and, therefore, not so subject to crowds of happy townsfolk. The only danger seemed to be from our own aircraft which, according to word of mouth reports, had already mistakenly attacked part of the convoy. For the first time, we displayed our yellow identification strips round the Company area. A rumour circulated that paratroops were to be dropped ahead of us to secure bridges along the centre line of the advance. But a high wind arose and continued for days, making an airborne operation unlikely. On the other hand, German opposition so far was negligible and the Irish Guards had not yet fired a shot in the advance.

Early next morning we set off from Douai, following the usual procedure. The company was ready to move and embussed at a certain hour, passing the company start point at another certain hour. From there the company took its allotted place in the main stream of battalion vehicles, proceeding to the brigade start point; each stage was marked by a halt of varying length. All this required detailed organisation, bearing in mind that for the most part we travelled on a single road, along which fuel, ammunition, food and water had to catch us up.

Information about what was happening elsewhere in the war was sketchy, but at least we learnt about the Allied landings in the south of France and of the tremendous American thrusts further south of us. Word came also from the Division about the capture by the Canadians and the 7th Armoured Division of flying bomb (VI) bases sited between us and the sea. This was of particular interest to many guardsmen whose homes in England lay in the path of the doodle-bugs. Never having been there before, my knowledge of the geography of Northern France and the Low Countries towards which we were moving was far from extensive, but I did my best to keep the platoon informed during our many roadside halts. It was important to break the monotony and keep thinking.

Leaving Douai, we set off for the Belgian border at high speed which slowed when we turned off on to cross-country cart tracks and fields. With their 4-wheel drive, the TCVs coped superbly. Their springing was so good that, although the chassis might tilt sideways at what felt like thirty degrees, the main body filled with nervous troops remained reasonably upright. Several times I thought we were going to tip over, and wound my window down for a quick exit, but each time we straightened up and all let out a sigh of relief.

Once in Belgium, the countryside changed. It was fairly flat in Artois, but it became even flatter now, with miles of ribbon development. At first, the local population gazed dully from the side of the road at the miles of convoy. But, in the industrial areas, the usual scenes of jubilation appeared, with a Belgian flag or two in almost every home. The speed with which the flags appeared implied a central distributing agency anticipating liberation, particularly as most of these black, yellow and orange flags were of a similar size, with an embroidered tassel hanging from the end of the pole projecting from a window.

Girls blossomed forth in eye-catching costumes of black blouse, yellow skirts and orange stockings. The colour scheme was startling, but no one cared. National expression was the theme. We were probably not more than an hour behind the armoured cars of the Household Cavalry in front, yet flags and costumes were ready and displayed for all to see.

We were pelted with flowers, fruit and blown kisses. Small boys amused themselves by hurling apples at any guardsman who did not duck in time. It paid to keep your eyes open. We flung out cigarettes and waved in return. Somehow it was difficult to realise that we were supposed to be at war. A small riot ensued when a large handful of cigarettes landed near a group of youthful resistance men. German rifles, Spandaus and ammunition belts were flung aside as the group dived to grab what they could.

Chapter 12

Entry into Brussels

It was 3 September, the fifth anniversary of the outbreak of war, when we left Douai and entered Belgium, making it a battlefield for the second time in five years. Our route lay through Athey, Enghien, and Hal, at the fastest pace so far, with halts few and far between. At one halt, the 2nd (armoured) Battalion Irish Guards roared past at a good 30 mph. The ground shook with the weight of the tanks and the wayside trees visibly trembled. A column of tanks travelling fast over a tarmac road is something to be seen and remembered.

Late in the afternoon, there was an 'O' Group meeting when we learnt that Brussels was the next stop. Each battalion was allocated its own sector. In the event, the Welsh Guards entered first. It was near 9 pm when the Irish Guards went in. Street lamps were lit for the first time in years (black-out no longer necessary). At first most of the population seemed to be still accustomed to the nightly curfew of the German occupation and remained indoors. Then, as the column rumbled on, people streamed out in their thousands, oblivious of the minor skirmishes where Germans attempted resistance. In one street, there might be flowers, lights, champagne and a delirious multitude, whilst round the corner there might be a bang and a crash as a German gun loosed off a shot before it was knocked out by a tank.

It was dark as we edged down the Avenue Louise between rows of trees, with a troop of IG tanks in front. A Belgian man ran alongside the TCV, leapt on the running board which doubled up as a mudguard, and told me in English that he had been an artillery officer until the collapse in 1940 when he had become a prisoner. He now wanted a weapon with which to kill Germans still holding out in the railway station. As we did not carry spare weapons for distribution, I gave him one of my two 36 (Mills) grenades, with a brief lecture on how to use it, hoping that he remembered there was only a four seconds' delay to the explosion after the lever was removed. From the Avenue Louise, we turned right, into the Forêt de la Soigne where we had been detailed to form a road-block at a crossroads. It was pitch black in the forest, with tall trees on either side.

A German anti-tank gun ahead of us fired and was engaged by our tanks in an exchange of fire for ten minutes. The 75-mm guns of the tanks thundered and crashed, whilst their Browning machine-guns criss-crossed the road ahead of us with tracer. We sat nervously in the TCV. If we debussed, there was a real risk in the dark of being shot or run over by the tanks. Donovan, the RASC driver, rooted round till he found his steel helmet under the seat. It was the only time I ever saw him wear it. Eventually, the skirmish ended and we continued past an upturned German 37-mm gun. A Spandau somewhere fired a prolonged burst high over the roof of the TCV as a parting gesture.

At the crossroads, my platoon was detailed to cover the most likely road, with our tanks about fifty yards behind us. Since sections placed either side of the road might kill each other if they fired indiscriminately, I allowed only certain slit trenches to fire, in prescribed arcs. Half an hour after arriving, whilst we were still digging in, there came the sound of a motor approaching up the road. I shouted to the sentry on the Bren and got everyone out of the way below ground. But the Bren never fired.

Desperate to stop the vehicle, which turned out to be a motor cycle, I stepped into the middle of the road and bellowed 'Halt'. The motor cycle slowed up and proved to have a side-car and three men: one driving, one pillion and one behind a large machine-gun in the side-car. At that moment I realised they were Germans; they recognised me as British and started to move. I shoved my revolver into the stomach of the German behind the machine-gun, who yelled to the driver to stop. The driver took no notice until a rifle butt hit him on the jaw. So with much muddling and some luck, we captured three Germans.

When I asked the sentry on the Bren why he had not fired, he said he had squeezed the trigger but nothing happened. He thought grit must have stopped the breech block. As he was an excellent gunner, I believed him. A week later, we knew we were both wrong.

By midnight, we were dug in, weary after ninety-seven miles in fourteen hours from Douai to Brussels. A platoon covered each of the three roads leading into Brussels at this crossroads, with a couple of sentries on the road coming out of the city. There came shouts from behind us, a crackle of shots, and a small truck that zigzagged round the tanks and accelerated down our road. When a Browning opened up from behind, we flung ourselves flat.

Standing up again, I got off four shots with my revolver and remember seeing the terror in the eyes of a young guardsman lying at my feet. He had recently joined us and not been under fire. As the truck passed the forward Bren guns, they both opened fire, catching it fair and square. It continued a short distance before stopping. What looked like a couple of figures melted into the blackness pursued by bullets.

A guardsman, who had joined us as a reinforcement only four hours before, had been shot through the fleshy part of the thigh. I left him to Sergeant Ennis and plunged into the forest after the Germans. A couple of collisions with tree trunks and one fall were enough to convince me that it was not worth it. It was more important to get the truck off the road where it blocked the field of fire. So we pushed it on to the verge out of the way, and examined the contents which turned out to be a mixture of silk stockings, women's clothes, boot polish, weapons and equipment. A stock of liquor I impounded, not trusting the platoon's thirst.

At 1 am another motor was heard approaching on our road. The deck was cleared for action and a reliable Bren with the sentry. The car drove straight into the converging fire of two Brens. Sparks flew off the road, glass tinkled and the car's tyres burst. I screamed to stop fire but one gunner insisted on emptying his magazine. One German escaped, whilst the other lay moaning in the road. When I approached, I found the last few bursts had practically severed the thigh of an officer of the Death's Head Division. It took half an hour to get him back to the Regimental Aid Post. Ambulances were unwilling to come forward after one had been fired on by a Spandau. The officer had apparently been returning from a party, unaware that Brussels had been liberated. He even had the unit's mail with him, all censored and ready for despatch, and a briefcase full of maps and documents. I grabbed his magnificent cap with the death's head insignia but unfortunately it was missing from my kit when I later returned to England. I've always regretted the loss of this souvenir.

The night was far gone, so I lay down for a brief spell, to be wakened by Alec who wanted my third section to go somewhere else. As we discussed this, there came another burst of firing from my platoon. Sergeant Ennis had caught a German staff car, killing the driver and Gestapo officer. An hour later, yet more firing showed a large truck careering past wildly before it finished up against a tree down a bank. Two Germans were hauled from the driving cab.

The back of the truck had its canopy tightly closed, so we shouted in German for the occupants to come out and put a bullet through the roof to hurry them up. But nothing happened. I climbed up but, hampered with a Sten, I had no spare hand to undo the canopy. Alec came to my help and asked me to cover him. He did not know that, being closest, I had heard the sound of whimpering. In a second, there was a rush from inside. Alec leapt out of the way as a couple of figures jumped down – two German soldiers, aged fourteen and fifteen, terrified out of their minds.

In the morning, our stretch of road looked like a scrap heap, with four wrecked vehicles, and pools of blood. The road surface was scarred where bullets had cut across. Some excitement arose when John Stanley-Clarke's platoon was found to be sited near an underground bomb dump, hidden in the forest. His concern was heightened when huge distant explosions echoed through the trees at intervals, presumed to be delayed-action charges in other dumps. A few civilians appeared, luckily without being shot by the sentry.

A distinguished-looking middle-aged man on a shining new bicycle produced papers and passport indicating that he was a Count and held a

British DFC from World War I. He was full of information about the Germans and reported the presence of three tanks about a mile away. Sure enough, we heard them approaching, causing the usual scramble to get below ground. The tanks stopped about 400 yards away with just their turrets showing over a rise in the road. They gave a few bursts of machine-gun fire which killed a guardsman climbing into his tank. They landed a shell in the road just outside my slit. Our own armament never got in a shot, as the tanks rapidly departed.

Chapter 13

Cheerful Brussels

In case there were any more Germans ahead of us, I took a patrol through the forest either side of the road, whilst a troop of Irish Guards tanks charged down the road at full speed. On foot, we crept forward in open order, moving from tree to tree, eyeing each dip in the ground as potential cover. Nothing happened.

At the end of the road, we entered a village and were immediately set on by a mob of enthusiastic well-wishers. Little flags were planted on us, hot mouths planted kisses, and a large bunch of grapes was pressed into my hand. They were beautiful sweet grapes. We took a lift back on top of the tanks, which had found as little as ourselves. The villagers streamed behind the tanks like the hunt behind the hounds. At our crossroads, a huge crowd had formed. We appeared to be the star turn for miles around. They stood round us watching every move, eager, happy and too delighted to take their eyes off us. They were even surprised to see us all shaving.

I had to double the sentries to prevent pilfering of equipment and ammunition. The locals tried hard to buy rifles from the guardsmen and rapidly cleared the area of German weapons and gear from the night before. The wrecked vehicles were stripped of tyres, seats, engine parts and anything that came unstuck.

The day wore on in chatter and animation. A smart horse-drawn coach appeared, driven by a coachman in a grey top hat. The owner dismounted in reverential silence and distributed bunches of superb grapes. A polished limousine, which somehow had petrol, drove up to the platoon and out stepped an elegantly dressed woman who produced four crates of bottles of alcohol which she said was for all the troops. I pushed my way forward and took charge of the bottles, to forestall finding myself with a platoon of helpless drunks. The lady went on to say she would present the officer with two bottles of Heidsieck champagne. When I said I was the officer, she looked surprised and obviously expected something grander. I never got the champagne.

In retrospect, it is possible that this display of opulence at the end of the German occupation might have arisen through doubtful friendships with the enemy and the lady was now making a public gesture to rehabilitate herself. There was the point that, in the German fashion, she insisted on treating the officer to something different. An ordinary person seldom differentiates – troops are just troops. She was clearly put out to discover the officer as dirty and dishevelled as his men.

On the other hand, I may have misjudged a genuine offer of help and appreciation. To give her credit, her alcohol was superb: rum, cognac, gin and liqueurs. I hid the bottles in the platoon truck and allowed one to be shared from time to time.

In the afternoon, four ragged men appeared, each supporting himself on a staff. They were French POWs who had escaped and were making their way back to France. Wearing only coats and trousers, they were pitifully thin, bearded, mere skin over bone, with feet in bad shape. Our stretcher-bearers treated them as best they could. We fed them and wished them Godspeed on their long trip home. Another ex-prisoner, a Belgian, came up demonstrating his voluble English which consisted largely of bad language learnt from his fellow-prisoners, Canadians.

In the midst of this, there was a crackle of shots, with people charging through the forest and women screaming. Prompt action on Alec's part saved a lot of firing at nothing in particular. Two things had happened at once. An anti-tank sergeant heard a noise in the bushes and thought he had found another skulking German – several had been seen. In fact, it was only another sergeant modestly relieving himself behind a bush. Further away, some townspeople had recognised a collaborationist and ran after her. These two incidents were magnified into a full-scale German attack, with all sorts of people out to shoot a Nazi.

The collaborationist, a pretty young girl, was later brought to me by a couple of guardsmen trying to protect her from the fury of the mob. I sat her on a bale of straw and waited for her panting and trembling to subside. White as a sheet, she rolled her eyes alarmingly. Her story (in English) was that she was a British subject (Belgian father, Welsh mother, and born in Cardiff), accused of being friendly with a youth who had since joined the German army. She claimed it was ridiculous to accuse her of sympathy with the Nazis. At this stage, she had snuggled up close to me, with her face ever nearer. Her hand rested on my knee. In the background, a grinning circle of guardsmen cheered me on. I looked at her papers. As large as life, they said she was married to a German officer. I passed her on to Alec, who sent her to the Civil Affairs Officer in Brussels.

In the evening, we had orders to hand over to the Welsh Guards and return to the Avenue Louise. They arrived four hours later and were shown the position in pitch darkness. As their company commander disapproved of our dispositions, they must have spent most of the rest of the night rearranging themselves. By coincidence, one of their platoon commanders was David Stevenson who took over my former position at the crossroads. In the Avenue Louise, we debussed for an unseen hot meal. As the officers stood talking, a shot rang out, striking sparks from the cobblestones beside Alec and me. It came from Guardsman Dolan in my platoon, who had got drunk on the sly and probably did not want any more war. I placed him in close arrest and took away his rifle, posing the problem of what should happen if we went into action, Fortunately, he later solved the problem for us by deserting.

We had apparently been withdrawn to the Avenue Louise because the CO was concerned about the battalion's transport parked there without protection from Germans who might unexpectedly appear. My platoon was set out and dug in at a small public gardens and a communal potato patch, all of which had so far been covered by a section of medium machine-guns of the Northumberland Fusiliers. They gleefully told us details of how they had fired that morning on a German emerging from a home: the first burst put three bullets through his head, one through his neck, and an odd one through his chest. I begged them not to open fire again on any account, as they were bound to kill us in their line of fire. Although nothing hostile occurred during the remainder of the night, it rained and soaked everyone.

The next day brought the crowds in real earnest. So much so that an important administrative point was brought into undue prominence. In the rural areas, the question of latrines was easily settled. Here, in a built-up area, it was a different matter. I sent out scouts and myself interviewed various smiling house-owners who were only too willing to let the officer use the toilet but not twenty or more men. One scout reported the presence of a nearby pub, which probably contained a public toilet. The lady in charge raised no objection and readily agreed not to supply the men with any alcohol. She was all smiles when she saw the ration biscuits and tins of bully beef that I gave her.

An extraordinary rumour began to spread amongst the crowds surrounding us. One and all claimed that Hitler was kaput; had left his headquarters and fled to Madrid; the *Wehrmacht* was in complete confusion and about to surrender.

My platoon did not believe a word of it. But it kept the crowds happy. They filled the Avenue Louise all day, cheering and shouting. A brass band paraded up and down followed by hundreds of young men and girls arm in arm, dancing and singing. It was like a riotous New Year's Eve, with screaming and shouting and people delirious with joy. Tank crews trying to carry out maintenance on their monsters were hugged and kissed. Some girls had an Irish Guards designation sewn on their shoulders, and a few wore khaki General Service caps. Even Sergeant Ennis sheepishly admitted several days later that he had mislaid his cap somewhere.

Battalion HQ found itself so pestered by the well-meaning throng that in the afternoon we shifted to the grounds of the King's Château at Laeken.

Checking upon my platoon before we moved, I was dismayed to find that we were one man short. As it turned out to be Dolan who had fired the shot on the previous night, I was secretly much relieved. But it led to trouble. Dolan was in close arrest, under the eye of a corporal. It appeared that the corporal had succumbed to the temptation of going to listen to a householder's radio tuned to an English broadcast by the BBC. He had assumed that Dolan was still in a drunken stupor. When the corporal returned, Dolan was gone. We did not bother to look for Dolan, being better off without him; in any case, he was likely to be picked up by the Military Police before long. But the corporal had to be placed under open arrest which was no doubt later allowed to lapse.

Chapter 14

Northern Belgium

No. 2 Company was allocated a distant position in a wood on the King's Château estate, well away from crowds and from Germans, too. Bobby Taylor, who had a knack of getting around, had made friends with a family in the Avenue Louise. He borrowed a motor cycle, with me riding pillion. His acceleration being particularly spasmodic at every halt, I was almost left standing in the air with my feet apart. But we had a much appreciated hot bath in his friends' house.

Next morning, 6 September, the Guards Armoured Division was on the move again. We drove out of Brussels through the Forêt de la Soigne and down the road to Louvain, which we raced through. I remember nothing of the place except that the cathedral was burnt out, leaving just the walls. From there, we continued to Diest, short of the Albert Canal, and stayed the night. The Welsh Guards group in front found the road bridge over the canal had been blown at Beeringen but the town was empty.

We halted for the Engineers to come forward and replace the bridge. The Division had by this time been organised into regimental groups, with one armoured and one infantry battalion of the same regiment working together. The various groups performed a series of leap-frogging movements, alternating with each other in the lead behind the armoured cars of the Household Cavalry who probed and pushed ahead along likely lines of advance.

At Diest, my platoon was detailed to guard a crossroads against interference from the flank. With the Division supplied for the most part along a single road from behind, it was vulnerable to flank attack and had already suffered in this manner. These flank attacks on the long thin line of communication were to become more frequent as we penetrated further into the Low Countries. But nothing happened to us and we sat in complete boredom beside a wrecked vehicle dump chatting to civilians.

A nervous elder of the community told me that on the previous day a group of German soldiers had finished a drunken party by hurling egg grenades at a passing Belgian family. He wanted me to dispose of two unexploded grenades. I gaily agreed, expecting the pins to be still in the grenades. On inspecting them, no pin was visible and it was apparent that they were unexploded blinds. Having promised to help, I could hardly back down, with a curious crowd watching me from a respectful distance. I should have chosen the best shot in the platoon and told him to fire at the grenades. But instead I pursued the stupid and useless course of getting someone to dig a hole, myself picking up the grenades by hand and putting them in the hole. It was reckless as I might have lost a hand and been blinded, and useless because it did not get rid of the danger; the grenades were still there for anyone to dig up deliberately or by mistake. I have never ceased to wonder at my luck in escaping serious and unnecessary injury from the silliest of actions.

Late at night, I was ordered to move the platoon in the TCV to Company HQ which was some distance away on the other side of the town. By this time, a few American soldiers in two Peep vehicles on a flank reconnaissance had joined the platoon but were unwilling to return whilst a force of German Tiger tanks was reported to be on their route. With these friends behind, we made our way in pitch darkness and the usual pouring rain to Company HQ where I was told to return again to our original crossroads.

This proved difficult. The approach to HQ had been along a one-way street, meaning that we could not retrace our steps on the same route. With only a sketchy idea of the alternative route, we found ourselves lost in open country. To turn a TCV without headlights might be asking for trouble. So I told Donovan to switch on the lights whilst I dismounted and guided him. We found the correct route by switching off the engine and listening for the noise of traffic, then aiming for it. Even then, there were problems as Engineers were travelling in the opposite direction with bridge-building apparatus that took up most of the road.

At the crossroads again, we slept for an hour or two until ordered before dawn to be on the move. This time I found two men short. A subdued hammering from a nearby horsebox revealed them. They had congratulated themselves on finding a dry spot out of the cold and rain but had not reckoned on the rain causing the woodwork of the door to swell until it refused to open from the inside.

The Bailey bridge over the Albert Canal had now been completed. We moved up to the south side, debussed and in the damp misty cold of the morning crossed the new bridge towards the town of Beeringen. Welsh Guards by the wayside shouted that the town was empty. As we entered the town, the sounds of a battle rang out, with small-arms, mortars and artillery explosions. A Spandau was firing from somewhere fairly close but not at us. A Welsh Guards tank rumbled rapidly into the main square, with flames leaping from its body. The platoon sheltered in doorways from bullets which were now hitting the upper parts of buildings. Wanting to know what was happening, I went forward to look for John Stanley-Clarke, whose platoon was ahead of mine, and found him and his platoon upstairs in a big building, shooting at Germans out of the window.

The battle continued spasmodically with the IG tanks firing across and along the canal past our side of it. Another company of the 3rd Battalion pushed down a side street, whilst the Welsh Guards swung off to the right from the main square towards Hechtel. No. 2 Company occupied the big building (a girls' school) but played no active part. We were not involved in street fighting and there was no direct German attack on us. The body of a dead German officer lay in the roadway. On this landmark, Alec Hendry gave me directions to move my platoon to take over the railway station. I had brought the platoon upstairs where there was more shelter from the heavy German shelling.

Now we set off down a side-street but had not gone fifty yards before a concentrated burst of shelling landed round us. Obviously a German

OP on a huge slag-heap ahead had seen us. We sought cover, myself in a narrow alleyway between two houses. Fortunately, there were no casualties. One shell that hit the house above me brought down a shower of tiles and glass; a long sliver of glass landed on my hand and stood upright between my knuckles, fortunately without causing lasting damage. This shelling unnerved the young guardsman who had looked so shaken at the firing in the Forêt de la Soigne in Brussels. He shivered and moaned piteously. Remembering how CSM Larking had dealt with this sort of thing in Normandy, I gave the guardsman no sympathy.

When the shelling stopped, we led on. Not knowing the way, I went myself some distance ahead, so that, if I took a wrong turning, there would be time to avoid the whole platoon getting into a tangle. We made a cross-country trip over gardens, walls and fences, still without finding the railway station. Peering round the corner of a house, I found myself looking at Lieutenant Ted Ryder who was about to do the same. This at least told me where the next-door company was but we were still no nearer the railway station.

Leaving my platoon under cover in a large house, I set off with my runner, Shackleton, to reconnoitre. At the corner of another home, I met Sergeant McElroy who had been in charge of the Brigade squad at the OCTU. This socialising was pleasant, although not in the best of circumstances. Eventually by the side of the road leading to the factory area ahead, I saw a railway line.

The station turned out to be merely a pair of buffers at the end of rusted rails, evidently having lain in neglect throughout the German occupation. The open ground in front stretched away for half a mile to a huge slag-heap, with a factory below, apparently occupied by the enemy. Strewn along the road leading to the factory were numerous German corpses, including a decapitated one. (This so offended one of the stretcher-bearers – who later had occasion to come forward – that he went out and removed it.)

A few civilians emerged from the cellars of the houses we were occupying and assured us that the war was over; they changed their tune next morning. On their information, we collected a couple of German wounded in a nearby house and sent them off for treatment. In our approach, we came across a dead Scots Guardsman lying on his back, with a small hole and patch of blood on the front of his tunic. As Sergeant Ennis had lost his steel helmet earlier, I persuaded him to take the dead man's, despite his obvious reluctance. He eventually accepted my argument that it was preferable to have a live platoon sergeant and overcome any feelings of distaste about using a dead man's helmet.

Having had nothing to eat since our compo breakfast nine hours earlier, we were hungry. Noticing a row of ripe tomatoes in the garden, I went out to gather some and was startled when Sergeant Cole rushed past me with rifle levelled, yelling, 'Look out, sir.'

I spun round, drawing my revolver, to be confronted by several German soldiers about fifteen yards away. Each held a white rag as a token of surrender, with hands in the air, crying, 'Ruski, Ruski' and 'Polski, Polski'.

We did not treat them kindly but sent them on their way unescorted back down the road where they flung themselves into a ditch with their hands over their ears when a salvo of German shells landed nearby. The platoon's view was that, if you wore a German uniform, you could not expect sympathy. I have since come to realise that this ignored the large numbers of men from occupied countries forced into the German Army against their will and only too anxious to desert – or surrender.

In the late afternoon, we had a grandstand view of another IG company attacking under cover of smoke across the open ground on our left towards the factory. The attack swept forward in great style, with plenty of support from medium machine-guns and tanks. But it came to a halt in the factory area, finding the task too much for a single company. Next morning, the Coldstream group came through us and began to mop up the factory. As they came past, I had a few words with Neville, one of their platoon commanders who had been part of our Brigade squad at the OCTU. A Coldstream Guardsman laden down under the weight of equipment, rifle and PIAT (Projector Infantry Anti-Tank) grinned momentarily and said, 'Well done, the Micks.' Remembering the days when, as a guardsman, I had carried one of these heavy weapons, I returned the compliment inwardly to a man able to be so cheerful under such a load. I hope he survived the heavy battle that the Coldstream fought in Beeringen.

During the morning, civilians appeared on the roads as if the battle was over. I repeatedly urged them to return to their cellars or at least remain within doors. They ignored the warnings and sadly paid for it. Alec Hendry and I were peering guardedly through a first floor bay window where I had posted a Bren gunner when there came a shattering explosion below us. In the road, a German shell had landed in the middle of a civilian family standing gossiping. At first, I did not realise this, being more concerned with my sentry across the road who had a gash in his thigh. He was shaken and horrified to find the backs of his hands a pincushion of tiny fragments of steel and splintered stone. (Apart from pain, wounded soldiers seemed to experience an initial mental shock at seeing parts of their body mutilated when seconds earlier they had been able-bodied.)

In the house opposite, a trail of blood led to the injured civilians. None of them was killed outright although the furthest from the explosion could not have been more than five yards away. An old man had a badly smashed leg and was fast bleeding to death. A small fair-haired boy had been hit in the stomach and in a few minutes lost all colour in his face and died. A girl aged about fifteen had shrapnel holes in her thigh. To deal with it, Corporal Russell (stretcher-bearer) lifted her dress, to the indignation of the girl's mother who kept pulling the dress down. I put a dressing on the arm of her younger sister who had a small hole in her arm. In no time, every neighbour from the vicinity braved shot and shell to crowd into the room to comfort the mother.

There were copious tears, much shouting, and obstruction all round, the worst being the local padre, a fat man difficult to circumvent at the best of times. These people, well meaning and badly shaken by the tragedy in the hour of liberation, got so much in the way and were such a nuisance pulling the girl's skirt up and down that I chased them all out of the room before despatching the injured in one of our ambulances.

At lunch time, I arranged for a corporal (the one under open arrest) and a guardsman to go to Company HQ and bring back the food. For some reason, they chose to go down the road instead of the safer but more arduous route through back gardens. They must have been seen for they immediately attracted a batch of German shells. The corporal was badly hit in the ankle, leaving a trail of blood down the road. With this trickle of casualties, the platoon was becoming a little smaller every day. It was sad to think of good men gone so easily. It emphasised the need to insist on every precaution against unnecessary casualties.

That afternoon my platoon was ordered to join another company as local protection for yet another crossroads whilst the rest of the Brigade passed through on its way to Helchteren. It was a long march down a straight tree-lined road past a burnt-out Humber scout car of the Household Cavalry. Later, in Roehampton Hospital in England, I met a Life Guards officer (recovering from the loss of an arm) who was the only survivor from a half-track vehicle that received a direct hit just outside Beeringen. Back at the crossroads, we dug in and passed the time till a hot evening meal arrived for the company I was with. At my request, my platoon was also fed. My own company now appeared, dropping off another meal to the platoon's delight; we all kept quiet about the earlier meal, but the truth came out later and caused awkward repercussions with the Quartermaster Sergeant.

Presently, I was ordered to shift the platoon position. This meant digging in a second time on another road. Late in the evening, the other company was ordered forward, leaving my platoon to cover the whole crossroads with a troop of tanks and to dig in for a third time. About midnight, the troop commander of the tanks received a wireless message, telling me and him to come and join a battle. It appeared that the advance to Helchteren had not gone well.

Chapter 15

Helchteren

It was pitch dark, cold and drizzling. We embussed in our TCV and followed the tanks. A Sherman tank is a big lumbering object in daylight but really quite elusive on a dark night without lights. We eventually reached what had been No.2 Company's position, but they were no longer there; we lay down in a couple of outhouses. No battle.

At two o'clock in the morning, I was woken to learn that my platoon was required to go forward to join No.2 Company ahead. The CSM, who had come to collect us, led us cross-country, laden down with containers of tea and food for the Company which had had no meal for some time. We duly staggered and crept at the same time, with bursts of small-arms fire somewhere in the vicinity. Unless tracer bullets are used, it is next to impossible at night to judge where fire is coming from or how close it is. The noise was quite considerable. I was in front behind the CSM when I heard the sound of a scuffle behind. It appeared that the guardsman with the bad nerves had dropped his container and was trying to flee when the platoon sergeant hit him on the jaw and told him to get on with it. It was a moment for me to look the other way.

We eventually found the squadron of tanks behind No.2 Company when I tripped over a figure asleep under a blanket. The tank men had no news of the situation except that it was unwise to go further forward because they were forced to fire at any sound ahead, in case of Germans with bazookas. This did not appear to be a happy arrangement for No.2 Company in front of the tanks. So I stayed where I was, spreading the platoon out in ditches, getting steadily colder and wetter. Presently, William Harvey-Kelly appeared in a great hurry to direct gun fire from the tanks on to his former platoon position which he had been forced to vacate. He said that Alec Hendry and Company HQ were in a farmhouse in the line of fire from the tanks' Browning machine-guns and dared not emerge. It was a comical situation. William brought a few unhappy prisoners with him, shaking with cold and fear. They were delighted when I told them to sit down, slapping their arms round their bodies to get warm.

All this time the sounds of a furious battle came from a hundred yards or more in front, with the tanks sweeping the ground ahead with tracer. Still no orders. An hour before dawn, during a lull, I crept forward with Shackleton, my runner, and found Alec under a table in his farmhouse. He told me to station my platoon across the road leading into Helchteren.

Returning to the platoon proved hazardous. The Brownings had opened up again, forcing us to cross a ploughed field face down along a furrow, with ricochets landing all round. We could see the tracer bullets hitting a nearby house and bouncing off in a slow arc, to bury themselves in the earth around us. I spread the platoon round a house with the utmost speed, as dawn was beginning to break and we did not want to be caught out in the open. On the first floor of the house was an abandoned German bazooka (called *Panzerfaust*) that must have accounted for the blazing Welsh Guards tank on the other side of the road. Dead Germans and weapons lay in the garden.

In the village of Helchteren ahead, the Welsh Guards were engaged in a fierce battle with what was understood to be a battalion of the Hermann Goering Division, both sides suffering heavily in the process. The Irish Guards Group was not involved, and my platoon spent the rest of the day resting and sleeping. Towards evening, we returned to the previous night's billeting area to embark in the TCVs and lead on across country, bypassing Helchteren. The route lay through a dense pine forest with a sandy floor. We spent a miserable night, very cold, with alternating rain and drizzle, and a thick ground mist. Orders were contradictory: sometimes warning us to be ready to move and other times to stand down.

The hot meal arrived about 2 am; with the usual difficulty in identifying tins and distributing them in the dark, I landed up (the officer eating last) with nothing but diced carrots.

In the early morning, we concentrated in an area of burnt-out heath near battalion headquarters and the vehicles. The plan was apparently to continue the advance across country, joining the main road somewhere ahead. This was all very well, but one guardsman in my platoon had somehow contrived to lose his rifle. Happily, the Regimental Quartermaster Sergeant was able to replace it. For the first time, we rode on tanks instead of in TCVs, clinging to the few handholds against the lurches and swaying of the tank. There was inevitably some competition for space behind the protection of the turret, meaning that I was generally in a more exposed position in front.

It required two and possibly three tanks to accommodate the average platoon. For most of us, it was our first close-up view of a tank. On reflection,. it seems surprising that, for infantry in an armoured division, training in Britain did not include any exercises in company with tanks. We had to be told on that particular day that, if an infantryman needed to speak to a tank crew, he should do so by means of the telephone set on the back of the tank. Otherwise, engine noise would make ordinary conversation inaudible. It did on the telephone, too.

We moved through the forest which echoed to the rumbling, clanking and squeaks of the tanks. About 9 am, we debussed in a large open stretch for the usual hang-about. The plan apparently was for a reconnaissance party to discover a suitable route ahead, adequate for tanks to cross the two or three streams that lay in our path. No.2 Company spread out in open order, ready to attack, whilst the recce party of tanks and infantry disappeared into the woods for most of the rest of the day. Confused firing and sounds of battle followed. Wireless reports spoke of opposition that was overcome, but no success in crossing the streams. Tanks had become bogged. The advance could not continue on this line.

Fortunately, the Grenadiers on the left reported a clear route to Hechtel. So the Commanding Officer obtained clearance from the Brigadier for the Irish Group to have priority over all other traffic, to lead the advance once more. We retraced our steps through the forest down the same sandy track which by this time was so churned up by tank tracks that it required the services of an armoured bulldozer, driven by a nonchalant untidy soldier, to level the three-foot deep ruts.

We eventually reached the road and the Grenadiers, passing several knocked-out German 88s and a Tiger tank with a gun projecting yards ahead of the tank itself. We overtook a long line of stationary support troops: 17-pounders, 25-pounders, SP (self-propelled) guns, engineering equipment. The guardsmen goggled enviously at the gun-tractors, festooned with bedding rolls, sheets of corrugated iron, chicken coops and other useful objects of near-civilisation. Front-line infantry of course possess only what they can carry on their backs.

The IG tanks swept on at a good pace, reaching a sandy plain dotted sparsely with trees. According to the map, it was the Belgian Army's artillery range. As we passed some buildings, the guardsmen on the tank ahead waved frantically at us but their shouts were inaudible over the engine noise. Fortunately, the sergeant in charge of my tank who was standing up in the turret shot his hand up in time to lift a telephone line clear of my head. It would otherwise have caught me by the throat. I had failed to see it, as the dust and wind had made my eyes sore. The next day I helped myself to a pair of German goggles, the dead previous owner having no further need.

Beyond the firing range, we joined a road and came upon an unusual spectacle on the side: a long row of boots and shoes dressed by the right. Nearby in the ditch were about fifty unhappy German soldiers, wriggling their stockinged toes in dejection, and guarded by a couple of stalwart Grenadiers. A little further on, we passed Peter whom I had last seen at the OCTU in Aldershot. The road had obviously been much used by the Germans. There were military signs every few yards, and enormous pits to hide tanks hull-down. At about six o'clock in the evening, tired and dishevelled, we clanked into the village of Exel.

The villagers greeted us warmly, scribbling messages in chalk all over the tanks. Normally, riding on a tank close to the open turret, I could pick up news from listening to the wireless messages relayed loudly, but this time we had no idea what was happening. So we stood uncertainly in a group, idly watching a fat girl climbing a lamp post at some risk to her modesty. I was just beginning to spread the platoon out in a defensive position, when Alec waved us back to the tanks again. We set off at a rattling pace down the road to Overpelt, passing en route armoured cars of the Household Cavalry covering all the side roads.

Chapter 16

Joe's Bridge

At Overpelt on 10 September, we debussed and, at the rear of the other two platoons in the Company, led off down the road to Groote Barrier, moving in single file up the hedge. After a couple of hundred yards, we found ourselves converging on the canal, a great broad sea of water. A few Germans were reported moving on the far bank. We passed a huge factory, with the sound ahead of German 88s and our own 75-mms crashing away, to a background of small-arms fire. We eased forward down a ditch, as a Spandau crackled on the left from somewhere on the distant slope of what looked like a slag-heap. Dusk was coming on and visibility lessening. An IG tank, beside which I was sheltering, swung its turret round to ninety degrees of the hull and fired its gun, nearly deafening me. The recoil caused the tank to sway alarmingly over towards me. Again, my otherwise excellent infantry training had not prepared me what to expect in close company with armour. A hundred yards further on, the road approached the canal again head-on, then turned left parallel with it.

Alec being away at an 'O' Group with the CO, Bobby Taylor (second in command) was in charge of the company. He had no specific orders except to capture the road bridge over the canal, so we just kept moving closer. To avoid advancing up the exposed road itself, we cut across the angle of the next corner behind a row of houses that sheltered us from any fire from the right.

Whilst waiting our turn to move, a worried Royal Engineers captain

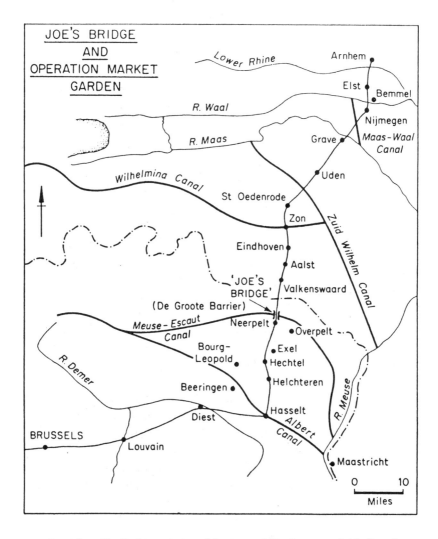

Reproduced by kind permission of Regimental Headquarters, Irish Guards

The Ever Open Eye

(later identified as Captain Hutton) came up to me and asked whether it would be safe to bring a truck up to the bridge (which at this stage we still could not see). I said that, in view of the noise of firing ahead, it would be unwise to do so. He departed and later brought forward on foot a group of four guardsmen ('volunteers' ordered by the RSM) to help him dismantle explosive charges on the bridge. He was rightly awarded a Military Cross.

Our route behind the houses was quite a steeplechase over walls and fences, stacks of wood, turf, coal and sawdust, through flower-beds and round air-raid shelters. It was enlivened by a Bren gun firing at us from some distant point on the left. We ignored it because the fire was inaccurate. It did cross my mind that a few return bursts into the air from our own Bren might have made the others aware from the sound that they were firing on their own side (the sound of Bren and Spandau fire being unmistakably different). A guardsman was slightly wounded by falling bricks where an armour-piercing shell from an 88 had gone through a house from front to back. In almost complete darkness, we reached a crossroads near the bridge which was like a fireworks display with shell bursts, tracer bullets and leaping flames from a burning house.

John Stanley-Clark, the leading platoon commander, had arranged for the tanks to provide covering fire to discourage action by the 88s on the other side of the bridge, whereupon a troop of tanks and the infantry platoon would rush the bridge. This was done and the bridge was captured, later being known as Joe's Bridge after the CO (Lieutenant-Colonel J.O.E. Vandeleur, always known as Joe).

I played no part in the action, having been ordered to stay in reserve until told what to do. After a while – and no orders – I set off with my platoon and met a group of shadowy figures. Challenging them, I was told, 'Commanding Officer's escort.' Another figure wearing a Canadian-type steel helmet and waving a German pistol approached and demanded to know who I was. I recognised the CO's voice. 'What the hell are you doing here? Get your platoon over the other side in double time.'

So I did.

On the far side, the road was embanked with a drop on either side; a

The Ever Open Eye

wood lay on the left and a house on the right. John Stanley-Clark and his depleted platoon were spread out on the right. I was told to clear the house and take over the ground just beyond it, ready for a counter-attack.

I had always prided myself on being able to reconnoitre a position in a hurry and set my platoon out in a defensive position in three to four minutes. This time I began by walking into a pond in the darkness, but found that the Germans had obligingly dug good trenches reinforced with tree trunks in exactly the positions that I would have chosen. We avoided the canal bank and footpath for fear they were mined, but next day so many civilians walked up and down them unscathed that it was obvious there were no mines. The house turned out to be a converted barracks for the German troops defending the bridge, with the night's guard roster listed on a blackboard.

Two unhappy German prisoners said they had arrived from Denmark only a few days earlier and had been overwhelmed by the speed of our advance, apart from the fact that they had been expecting their own, not British, tanks. Their 88 guns were designed for anti-aircraft work and so lacked shields for the crew who had no chance against heavy Browning fire from the IG tanks. Although wired for demolition, the bridge had not been blown, because the sergeant in charge had departed at the first sounds of battle, omitting to fire the charges. The officer had preceded him, removing all transport and so marooning the gun crews.

There was no counter-attack during the night, but next morning fighting flared up on the other side of the bridge where German armour, including a Tiger tank, had suddenly appeared and caused some damage around Battalion HQ before being beaten off. The rest of the day was spent in improving our positions. I was inside a small brick hut and was busy cleaning my Sten when there was the familiar rumble of a tank outside, followed by the collapse of the wall and doorway. The back of a tank projected through. When it moved away, I emerged in a hurry, to find that the driver of the Firefly was unaware that he had touched the building at all.

Joe's Bridge was about two miles from the Dutch border, with flat countryside of largely sand and fir trees. At this point, the Escaut canal was some fifty yards across with pebbled sloping banks, running dead straight. On the far side, towards the factory, were cranes, wharves, and loading basins. Civilians were stopped from crossing the bridge, for fear that the Germans were likely to dress in civilian clothing and blow up the bridge which was vital for the continued advance.

We wondered why we were sitting still. Having captured the bridge against minimal opposition, it would be reasonable to suppose that the advance would continue at once, keeping up the momentum and not giving the Germans any time to organise defence. According to the *History of the I.G. in the Second World War*, Lieutenant-General Horrocks (Commander 30 Corps) came up to the bridge on 12 September and told Battalion HQ that there would be 'no move for the Guards Division before the 16th' with the IG leading the advance; I was not invited to meet the General. In due course we learnt about Operation Market Garden which was intended to be a land-based advance by the GAD from Joe's Bridge on the Escaut canal to Arnhem and beyond. This advance would be helped by airborne landings in Holland to capture important road bridges ahead of the GAD: American 101st Airborne around Eindhoven; American 82nd Airborne around Nijmegen; British 1st Airborne around Arnhem.

In practice, Operation Market Garden did not start till 17 September. From 11 to 16 September, the GAD sat immobile for six whole days, giving the Germans ample time to organise defence. The delay apparently arose because the Chiefs of Staff, with the enthusiastic backing of pushy airborne generals, had decided on an airborne operation, partly to make use of the large airborne forces sitting unused in Britain and denied action in repeated cancellations of earlier operations. The earliest that Market Garden could be mounted was 17 September.

No convincing reason has ever been given why the GAD could not have continued to advance from 11 September on the day after the capture of Joe's Bridge, with the airborne operation taking place from 17 September.

This might have ensured a link-up at Arnhem road bridge by 18 September, the airborne having been assured that they would be expected to hold the bridge for not more than forty-eight hours. It may not be too far-fetched to say that the GAD might even have captured the bridge themselves before the airborne arrival.

There have been claims that the six days' delay was also necessary to allow supplies of food, fuel and ammunition to reach the GAD and other units of 30 Corps up the long thin line of supply which from time to time was disrupted by German attacks from the flanks. But the supply situation was never desperate; short at times but not even approaching the stage where the GAD could not move another yard without fresh supplies. It is hard to believe that a more realistic and resolute mind in the highest command would not have insisted on the GAD's pressing on regardless and keeping up the momentum of the hitherto rapid advance. If necessary, air drops of supplies could have been organised. Instead of that, a priceless opportunity was thrown away. The war at that stage was very far from won, and it was wrong to assume that the Germans were incapable of further organised defence.

Back at the bridge, on 12 September, a battalion of Coldstream infantry passed through the two companies of IG and took up positions about a mile from the Dutch border. On the next day, 13 September, the Welsh Guards took over our positions whilst we moved further left into a pine forest. No.2 Company was given the task of local defence for Battalion HQ. The news turned sour when we discovered that, in addition to digging our own slit trenches, we were expected to provide them for HQ personnel as well. In the evening, Bobby Taylor took me in a jeep to the factory for a wash (my first since Brussels). We climbed perpendicular ladders and wended our way between lathes, belts and machine benches to dressing rooms and showers, all clean and well provided in separate cubicles. It was a real pleasure, spoilt slightly by a blocked drain and flooded floors.

That evening there was sporadic shelling of our perimeter, indicating that the Germans had discovered our position and were reacting. Just before dark, a roaring noise in the distance disclosed a German aircraft like a training plane. It circled the bridge and dropped a couple of bombs that missed. Mobile Bofors guns mounted on the backs of trucks round the bridge opened up but not before the aircraft had made several runs over the target.

Early next morning, the sound of small-arms fire developed on our left. It appeared that a German counter-attack was in progress against No.3 Company along the edge of the forest. Because of the thickness of the trees, it was impossible to prevent some enemy infiltration. Around Battalion HQ, we had little to do except sit and listen to the din some hundreds of yards away. I was ordered to send one of my sections to help No.3 Company, so I detailed Sergeant Sullivan and his five men to accompany Humphrey Kennard and his platoon; he had also been ordered forward in support. In half an hour, Humphrey had been killed and I never saw my section again.

I learnt later that the section had been placed more or less in the path of the main German attack. At the crucial moment when the Germans came into view, the Bren gun jammed and the section was overrun. This was the same gun that had jammed in Brussels on the first night when the German motor cycle combination came down the road. At that time, the very experienced corporal in charge of the gun had said the jamming must have been caused by grit in the breech block; tried later, the gun had worked perfectly.

A long time later, I heard that most of the section were taken prisoner, but the guardsman with bad nerves whom the Platoon Sergeant had forcibly restrained earlier on was killed. The unfortunate man should never have been posted as a guardsman. He might have served a useful purpose in some job behind the front.

Casualties came back on foot to the nearby Regimental Aid Post, with the dazed and bewildered look that a wounded man often takes on. German shelling came closer to Battalion HQ, but nothing direct, despite the presence of the 3-inch mortar platoon firing from immediately behind us. Our own IG tanks had been withdrawn for maintenance and replaced temporarily by a Hussar regiment.

From some distance down the canal, a German gun fired towards the bridge for the better part of three hours, without apparent hindrance from the Hussars. My irritation with them increased when a particular tank drove all over my platoon's slit trenches which were our battle positions; the platoon itself was hidden in the woods to avoid giving away our position. With the trenches caved in, I went forward to complain to the driver, to be met by a highly polished Lieutenant-Colonel clambering down. The words died in my mouth.

Chapter 17

Night Patrol

Towards evening the German shelling grew heavy, with air bursts overhead in shattering explosions, making us keep our heads well down in the slit trenches. During a lull in the firing, Alec came round and told me to get ready for a patrol that night. No.3 Company had been forced to retire some distance to a closer perimeter, and the object of the patrol was to discover whether the Germans were still in front or had retired. Information from prisoners was that two battalions of German paratroops, fitted out with new equipment, weapons, uniforms and underclothes, had been employed in the attack on No.3 Company but had not succeeded. This was hard to believe. One reinforced company could hardly withstand such a weight of fire from two battalions.

Before the next bout of shelling, I doubled forward towards No.3 Company and found them lining the edge of the wood, with a clear 600 yards of flat open ground in front, stretching to another wood. My job was to search for German presence in the right hand corner of the opposite wood. The alternative approaches were either along the canal and up through the wood – dismissed as too noisy and difficult in the dark – or straight across the open and trust to luck. Taking a compass bearing, I warned the forward troops of the impending patrol and retraced my steps. On the way, I met Guardsman Piercey who had shared the scrape in the lane with me on that memorable 11 August at Sourdeval. We greeted each other warmly, he still as cheerful as ever, despite a nasty time earlier in the day during the attack on No.3 Company.

I walked straight into another bout of shelling, fortunately further ahead where the trunks of the trees might provide some protection. A loud whine coming my way caused me to bury my face and the muzzle of the Sten in the pine needles, as a chunk of metal crashed through the trees overhead.

Back with No.2 Company, I met John Blake, the Pioneer officer, with whom I had shared a room at Hobbs Barracks, Lingfield. He told me he had been out the night before, blowing up a bridge over a tributary feeding the canal. Then, in the early morning, he had gone for a walk and, hearing a noise on the other side of a hedge, had found two German soldiers sitting behind a machine-gun. He shot the NCO through the head but had to retire in a hurry ahead of a hail of bullets. It sounded an extraordinary story but I knew him of old and quite believed it. He took a deep interest in all enemy weapons and explosives, possessing no less than ten pistols and an adapted German rifle. Sadly, I later heard that he lost his right hand in a training accident.

My patrol was due to set out at 11 pm, thus giving time for a meal. Despite our proximity to the front, the company officers ate in their own mess, a bivouac. As I sat down to a tin of meat and vegetables (M&V), the shelling started again, resulting in a mad rush to the nearest slit trenches. The one I reached rapidly filled with officers and guardsmen, the top man in the heap having little more than his head under cover. 'Jerry smelt the scoff and must be putting over a few to keep the Micks hungry,' he remarked in an unconcerned voice.

Without a meal, I returned to my platoon where Sergeant Ennis, the platoon sergeant, held a ballot to choose the two men to accompany me; I rejected both as unsuitable. To my surprise, Guardsman Shackleton (a former officers' mess waiter and always looking for adventure) offered his services, together with the 2-inch mortar man, a tall taciturn pillar of strength. Alec reminded me of our own artillery and 3-inch mortars, both of which I had forgotten. As they were due to put down harassing fire for most of the night in roughly the area where I would be, Alec arranged for them to switch to targets elsewhere.

With mud-darkened faces, we set out in the pitch black. The approach to No.3 Company took longer in the dark, and it was important to reach the exact spot where I had taken the compass bearing that afternoon. On warning the sentry about our patrol, he told me to watch out for the wire in front and the trip flares; the Bren gunners had orders to fire immediately a flare went up. No one had warned me about this. The compass bearing was 355° which is near enough to due north for most practical short distances. We slipped past the front line and headed out into the darkness of sand, heather and rank grass.

Luckily, there was no moon, nor was the sky at all luminous. The only danger lay in being silhouetted against the horizon, but this was minimised by a ground mist.

We started out with the intention of crawling as near the German end of the wood as possible, but after about a quarter of an hour I grew heartily tired of it. The use of muscle and all one's senses at night was quite exhilarating. We stood up and walked the rest of the way, avoiding ditches and gullies where there might be trip wires. Despite Alec's request to the artillery, a batch of 25-pounder shells passed over our heads into the wood ahead. They make a different whistle in flight to the German 105 mm, being more drawn out as if it were about to stop, which it doesn't. Away on our left, a Bren and a Spandau were engaged in a lengthy duel.

After an hour of movement, I grew seriously perturbed about our position. We had followed a belt of soft sand in order to make less noise. By my reckoning, we ought to be practically in the wood, yet there was neither sight nor sign of it. Moving on, we skirted a burning farm, crossed a road and found another burning farm. I was really worried. It had looked so simple in daylight; just a straightforward compass march, and here we were amidst burning farms that certainly had not been there during my reconnaissance of the afternoon.

We sat down for a rest whilst I did some thinking; the other two were not aware of my doubts. I came to the conclusion that the farms must have been shelled after my reconnaissance, and because I had not seen them they must be further to the right of the wood. Following the soft sand must have led us too far to the right. Our position ought, therefore, to be opposite or slightly beyond the end of the wood, having regard to the hour and a half that we had been walking. The obvious thing to do now was to swing left and come up behind the wood.

A scuffling noise came from the nearest farm. Before I could stop him, Shackleton had gone off to investigate. It was unwise of him, as the less anyone knew of our presence, the better. Luckily, it turned out to be only a bewildered calf trapped in a shed. Shackleton set it off in the direction of the Germans but it turned off, probably looking for food and drink in more familiar surroundings.

Moving slowly, I could now see the wood about 150 yards ahead, a long low blur against the ground mist. We crawled closer in short bounds, listening intently. At about twenty-five yards from the edge of the wood, we lay flat for some time. I think all three of us fell asleep. We had been out for some two hours and it was after 1 am. The spell was broken by the sound of voices in front. It appeared that a German sentry ahead was complaining that his relief was late in coming to take over. I knew enough German to be sure that it was the enemy. Since there was no doubt that the Germans were still there, we had fulfilled our task and it was time to make our way back. We returned slowly, as it is the most dangerous part of a patrol. Nearing our own lines, I whistled loudly to attract attention. Closer still, I whistled again, to be on the safe side.

To my delight, my reciprocal compass bearing brought us back to within five yards of where we had set out. Moving through the trees back to No.2 Company was a matter of creeping along with a hand in front and a cautious foot against falling into a slit trench. I sent the two guardsmen to bed whilst I reported to Battalion HQ which was sited down a huge roofed-over dug-out and filled with sleeping signallers and runners. Captain Eric Udal, the Intelligence Officer, wirelessed my news to Brigade HQ which expressed some surprise as they expected a counter-attack from a different direction. Next morning, an unarmed burial party from the IG reported the wood clear of Germans. I stick by my ears that I distinctly heard people speaking German twenty-five yards away. It was of course possible that the Germans withdrew after my patrol had departed.

In the morning, an advance party from another infantry division looked over our positions, preparatory to their taking over. I sat down to a large meal of bully beef and champagne for breakfast, having missed dinner on the previous night. (The champagne came from German stocks discovered by Captain Lord Carrington, Grenadier Guards, in a warehouse in Brussels and distributed to every battalion in the Division.) The shelling had stopped for the time being. It had caused only one casualty in the company, but had damaged the roof of the 3-ton cooker truck.

At midday, we withdrew on foot to the bridge which by now was somewhat battered. A group of Sappers was busy hammering planks over the holes caused by the German SP gun. To one side, a Bailey bridge was being pushed across from a temporary ramp. We tramped back to the factory area, passing en route the infantry battalion replacing us. They looked at us a little wonderingly but not more than we did at them. It was noticeable how much smaller than guardsmen most of them were. One particularly short man was lumbered with a PIAT, the heaviest weapon in a platoon.

At the factory, we embussed in TCVs. Donovan, the RASC driver of my TCV, complained that the platoon bicycle had disappeared when he left it unattended for a few minutes amongst a crowd of civilians. I was annoyed with him, as it was quite obvious what would happen. People subject to severe shortages for years are apt to help themselves when the opportunity arises.

We were due for a rest in a little village that straggled along a main road in the usual ribbon development of Belgium. It was now 15 September, four whole days after the capture of Joe's Bridge. Everyone was perturbed by the delay in the advance and could not understand it. Admittedly, much of the rest of the Second Army was somewhere behind us, but every day of inaction would probably result in greater opposition ahead. This became only too apparent in the days to come. There was, of course, a danger of our being cut off by interruption of the long thin line of supply. But subsequent events showed that the risk in continuing the advance at once might have been justified.

On 16 September we had a day of rest. My platoon was billeted in a barn, but a number of men prepared to sleep in the open under German groundsheets fastened together to make a tent. No.3 Company, which was depleted after its battle in the past few days, was divided up amongst the other three companies, so that the battalion was reduced to a three-company basis, an advantage in some ways when riding on the tanks of the three-squadron 2nd (armoured) battalion IG. At this stage, the officers were summoned to Battalion HQ. There was idle speculation that we might all be awarded medals, after helping to capture the bridge (John Stanley-Clark had received the immediate award of a Military Cross). Nothing of the sort. On behalf of Regimental HQ in London, the Adjutant wanted to know whether officers on a Hostilities Only commission wished to seek a permanent commission after the war, assuming they survived. I declined the offer.

An 'O' Group in the morning gave us the news that, at 1435 hours next day (17 September), Operation Market Garden would start, with the IG Group leading the advance straight up the road to Eindhoven, Nijmegen, Arnhem and the Zuider Zee. Supporting the advance would be ten regiments of field artillery, four of medium, and one of heavy. In addition, there would be eleven squadrons of rocket-firing Typhoon aircraft circling overhead, ready to deal with opposition.

The plan envisaged the Guards Armoured Division advancing on a one-tank front for over 100 miles. The generals apparently considered this to be realistic, bearing in mind that, as part of the Operation, there would be airborne landings ahead to secure road bridges. The infantry division which had joined us a couple of days before was to move along either side of the road to a depth of roughly 200 yards. The IG infantry would advance riding on tanks on the road. It was, therefore, important that the supporting fire should not damage the road.

Chapter 18

Operation Market Garden Starts

The morning of 17 September was spent loading vehicles, checking equipment and weapons, and the dozens of administrative details that crop up at such a moment. The platoon truck (15 cwt) was so full that it could scarcely take another toothpick on board, being filled with blankets, greatcoats, respirators, large packs, spare ammunition, tripods, spare tyres, tools etc. There were even items tied across the roof.

At midday, we embussed in TCVs and moved haltingly forward past the successive start lines, finally stopping in the artillery region as the barrage opened up. The noise was deafening, so much so that I was unable to make myself heard. Great sheets of flame flashed from the muzzle as the whole gun jumped in the air from the recoil like a baboon on all fours. There was a continuous roar from the further batteries, punctuated by thunderous blasts from the nearer, the whole causing one's wits to become confused. The leading company overtook us on foot as it made it way up to the first squadron of tanks.

At 1430 hrs we crossed the bridge over the canal and continued in convoy to a point beyond where the leading Coldstream outpost had been. Here we waited. No.2 company was second in the order of march, with Battalion HQ and a large number of tanks in front. The thunder of the barrage never halted, with the range lifting every two minutes. Along the sides of the roads were shallow shell craters, blast-marks blazing the trees and whitening the asphalt. Browning machine-guns rattled ahead, in the direction of tall pillars of greasy black smoke indicating where

The Ever Open Eye

tanks were on fire. It became only too obvious that our worst fears were realised and that the easy advance envisaged by the planners was a pipedream.

The Germans had placed infantry with bazookas close to the road, whilst 88s were hidden further away in the edges of the woods. By knocking out the second troop of tanks, the first was trapped, unable to retire down the blocked road or to advance or to deploy off the embanked road. There was a heavy loss in tanks and crews. Further back on this single road, No.2 company still sat in TCVs, prepared to debus but not yet wanted.

We watched with detached interest the Devons and the Dorsets on either flank advancing in extended order, lying down, getting up, doubling forward, and firing. The innermost men were only ten yards from the convoy where we sat in soft-skinned vehicles in the long line of transport. It seemed either unnecessary bravado on our part or excessive caution on theirs; perhaps a bit of both.

Guardsman Magee, the driver of the Bren carrier, reported figures on the right behind a hedge. As we were now ahead of the infantry battalion on that side, the figures could only be Germans. The Browning on the carrier opened up with a clatter, and the Bren gun sentries on watch through the roof openings of the TCVs joined in, too. The other two Bren gunners in each platoon also jumped out to have a go. In the end, there were eight Brens and one hopeful Sten firing away.

The convoy moved forward spasmodically when the leading troops managed to advance. On either side, isolated farms and haystacks burnt furiously as the Hussar regiment shot up anywhere that might hide German troops, guns, or observation posts. Lightning aircraft with their twin booms twisted down from their formation, turning round and round like sharks after elusive prey. Their machine-guns crashed out, often from far behind us with the tracer passing over our heads in a shallow angle towards the ground. The Thunderbolts and Typhoons, controlled by an air liaison officer with Battalion HQ, fired rockets in continuous succession.

Each aircraft in turn flew down the road, releasing its rockets in a cloud of black smoke from some distance behind us. The rockets passed overhead with a whine descending the scale. Before the explosions of the first batch had cleared, the second batch was on its way. The whole picture was one of overwhelming power and destruction, complete with a shattering noise. All the while, our own artillery barrage passed overhead, whistle after whistle almost lost in the general din.

When a second line of traffic drew up alongside us, the confusion became too much and we were at last ordered to debus and advance on foot. We all felt safer. A fat Falstaffian figure with white hair, an inadequate beret, and a camera slung round his neck came towards us on foot from the opposite direction. I hailed him for news and was treated to a prolonged stare that rested finally on the stars on my shoulders. With the air of an old campaigner, he grunted, 'Pretty hot up there,' putting the emphasis on the last word and pointing towards the front. This was my only contact with a war photographer.

Unescorted prisoners, with their hands folded behind their heads, began to appear down the road from the front, their coats flapping as they ran with that curious shambling gait of the physically frightened. They lurched from side to side with the effort of keeping their hands unnaturally behind their heads. At a Regimental Aid Post by the roadside, a batch of them sat in the ditch smoking and laughing. When they sniggered at a bewildered Devon soldier nursing a bloodsoaked hand, they were nearly murdered where they sat.

A rumour passed down the line that a prisoner with his hands up had thrown a grenade into a Bren carrier. In a minute or two, we passed a carrier flaming furiously, likewise the 6-pounder anti-tank gun that it had been towing. A dead German lay by the roadside.

All at once, the crust of the opposition broke and we embussed again in the TCVs, without having taken any part in the battle. The Dutch border had been crossed at about 3 pm and it was now late afternoon. According to the battle plan, we should have been well into Holland by now. Clearly things were not going to plan.

At one point, the 4-wheel drive TCVs left the road and detoured through a hedge, two ditches and a piece of very rough ground to avoid five brewed-up Sherman tanks on the road. A baled out crew had passed us earlier, unmistakeable with their strained eyes, screwed-up faces and extreme haste to make for the rear.

In the midst of a wood, five guardsmen and Ted Ryder (he had supervised the Young Officers course on my first arrival at the IG Training Battalion, Lingfield) suddenly appeared beside us, with Ted waving a pistol. I halted the truck and gave him a lift. He had been the leading platoon commander in the advance and had lost the tank under him from a direct hit. He thought that the five guardsmen with him might be all that was left of his platoon. He was in a hurry to catch up, in case any more of his platoon were still there. He told me Cyril Russell had been wounded.

We debussed again in a long stretch of open road, facing an abandoned 88 gun on the road. A tank crew went to immobilize it but succeeded instead in firing it by mistake as they were trying to remove the breech block. Fortunately, it was facing towards the Germans. Unfortunately, the recoil caught a guardsman in the face and shoulder, breaking his nose. It was growing darker with a peculiar luminous glow behind the clouds piling up on the horizon. It was quiet too, with little or no firing. Once a burst of Spandau fire sent us scurrying into the deep ditches either side. During a lull I went to look at an overturned German 35-mm anti-tank gun. Alongside it was another small gun on wheels, looking like one of the pieces used to start yacht races.

Chapter 19

Valkenswaard & Southern Holland

Unescorted prisoners continued to come doubling down the road, trying to find someone who wanted them. Some were shaking with fear, and possibly reaction from the effects of the pounding by shells, rockets, and machine-gun fire. We greeted them with loud yells to encourage them on their way. Most of them were paratroops in camouflage smocks, with heather fastened to their helmets. One burly German had a red and yellow medal ribbon. For service in Russia, he told me.

For the last stage to the town of Valkenswaard in south Holland, we rode in pitch darkness on tanks, crowding on because there were fewer tanks after the battle. Over the radio, I heard Lieutenant-Colonel Joe giving orders in his usual forthright manner and cancelling a heavy artillery shoot on the town 'because you're too bloody slow'. Just as well, as there proved to be little or no opposition there and a heavy bombardment of the town would have killed more civilians than Germans.

The aircraft had departed at dusk, to our relief, as the last burst of machine-gunning from the air had apparently landed amongst our leading company. My tank's radio carried a running commentary from the front troop commander as he entered Valkenswaard a few miles ahead of us. His reluctance to penetrate too far in the dusk into an unseen built-up area was equalled by the insistence of his commanding officer to get a move on.

Shortly before the town, the tank I was riding on approached a bridge reported to be in poor condition. It had apparently been damaged in 1940 and rebuilt on a new line with an embankment on either side. In the dark, with no lights showing, it was hard to see the road and more so for the driver down in his compartment. He failed to follow the exact course of the tank in front and veered slightly to the right where the ground dropped away some three feet. The tank lurched to its right and stopped at an angle of forty-five degrees. We on top leapt off as far as we could to avoid the tank landing on us. Fortunately, the only injury was to my servant, Glendinning, who strained a wrist.

The big question was what to do next. The tank tracks just scraped the ground futilely and it looked as if it would need to be towed back on to the road. As the rest of my platoon was somewhere ahead on other tanks, we had to get a lift, spurred on by the CO who passed at that moment shouting his usual instructions to get a move on. This was easier said than done. My yells to passing tanks were unheard above the engine noise and I was unseen in the dark, so dare not stand on the road and wave. A half-track stopped for a moment, but when I stuck my head in the back to ask for a lift I was told the CRA (Commander Royal Artillery) on board was not going to stop and I should get the hell out of the way.

After about ten minutes, the tank commander called me back. I don't know how they did it in so short a time but the crew had piled up a ramp of stones and earth in front of the tank track. With a great lurch, the tank climbed up to the road, narrowly missing another vehicle level with it. We clambered on top again and made for the town. Once in the streets, we followed the stream of vehicles which thinned out as we reached the central square.

Debussing, I walked round for a minute or two till I met some of No.2 Company and located the rest of my platoon which Sergeant Ennis had set out in a defensive position. There was the usual scene of spades clinking as slit trenches were dug, equipment laid aside, and the sentry behind his Bren gun. The company held the north side of the square, covering a number of roads and an inconveniently placed church. Not liking Sergeant Ennis's disposition, I rearranged the platoon, taking in a couple of houses. My experience of shelling was that the ground floor of a house offered the best protection, so I tried as far as possible to put men indoors, posting the Bren in bay windows.

The square was a bustling confusion of shouts, digging, engines roaring. In the centre was a bandstand surrounded by a patch of grass, making a convenient parking place for tanks. By morning, the area was a desolation of smashed fences, ruined flower beds, deep ruts and not a blade of grass anywhere. A few Germans were held in the bandstand, bewildered by the sudden arrival of tanks. The local cigar factory was burning furiously, as were a few houses, sending showers of sparks in the air. I had never seen a building on fire before and was quite fascinated. Nothing could be done to put out the fire which continued to burn, casting light and shadow widely. There was a constant roaring of wind and flame, a crash of walls collapsing and glass breaking.

A guardsman told me that the company had shot up a German horse and cart as it entered the town (a lot of German transport was horse-drawn). About fifty yards away near a burning house lay a body. I went over to have a look and, as I bent over the body, the man opened his eyes, moaned, said, '*Sehr krank*,' and relapsed. He appeared to have a serious stomach wound. I arranged for stretcher-bearers to remove him, although I doubted whether he would survive.

From the moment we had entered the town, the civilians had shown the usual signs of rejoicing at their liberation. In practice, their presence was a nuisance, standing in groups round every soldier, hunting for souvenirs (kit had to be guarded), insisting on shaking hands and buttonholing the officers for news of Queen Wilhelmina and Prince Bernhard. When a civilian with an air of consequence appeared, wearing a multi-coloured armlet and a beret, I took the opportunity to ask him (he spoke good English) to tell the civilians to stay indoors, as there might be heavy casualties among them if the Germans started to shell the town. I remembered particularly what had happened at Beeringen on the Albert Canal when civilians had crowded the streets.

The civilian harangued the crowd, but it had little effect when someone looked in the German wagon and discovered it to be loaded with crates of butter, bread, sausages, flour, potatoes and boxes of cigars. In five minutes, the entire load had disappeared. Individuals hurried off with armfuls and cries of joy. I collected a few loaves of gingerbread for distribution among the platoon; we had not eaten for some time.

After this things became quieter. Platoon Headquarters had been installed in a well-to-do residential house, presided over by a fattish, but pretty young woman who was kissed at intervals by the two men on the premises. My turn never came round. I was too tired in any case, falling asleep in a chair until woken by Glendinning with some hot food that had just arrived. This was followed by a visit from Alec Hendry, ordering me to take my platoon to reinforce No.3 Company which had just been charged by a number of German half-tracks at the other end of the town.

Putting on my equipment again, I rounded up the platoon and tramped across the town. At the road-block that we were supposed to take over, the NCO there said he had received no orders and was happy to remain where he was. He then promptly tripped over a tree trunk lying across the road but steered me round a rocket head that had apparently failed to explode from the afternoon's air strike.

To resolve matters, I left the platoon there and made my way to No.3 Company HQ. The officers had obviously decided that there was no further threat. They had just finished dinner and invited me to join them. The bottles were empty, however, and I declined as this was not a moment to be convivial.

Since No.3 Company did not require our services, I returned to the platoon and we made our way back to No.2 Company HQ to report the news to Alec. He was absent, so I sat down outside the door and waited half an hour for his return. He had been reconnoitring the town. Eventually, I was allowed to go back to the former position, followed by a stumbling line of tired guardsmen. It was 3.30 am and much quieter; the fires had burned low.

The kissing lady was surprised to see us back again, especially as I had rung the front doorbell instead of breaking a window to get in. Outside, on the edge of the road was a section of medium machine-guns (Northumberland Fusiliers) that I had helped to position earlier in the night. They had accepted my suggestion willingly, as it merely meant occupying the slits that we had partially dug. In front I had dragged the empty wagon across the junction of three roads as a makeshift barricade. Rather it had been the horse that did the dragging, under the management of Guardsman Donoghue who in civilian life worked in a stable. He had calmed the frightened horse and then rode it up and down bareback, delighted to have a chance to ride again.

The rest of the night, such as it was, passed uneventfully. In the early morning, unshaven, dirty and still tired, we packed up ready to move. The transport had crowded into the square and was overflowing down the road to Eindhoven. We bade goodbye to our involuntary hosts, with the kissing lady escorting me to the door as if I were an honoured guest instead of a tiresome nuisance. Embussing in the TCVs, we sat waiting for the day's advance.

It is a sad reflection that we should never have stayed the night in Valkenswaard but should have continued to advance all night to Eindhoven and beyond nonstop. Having broken the crust of German opposition on the first day of Operation Market Garden and achieved surprise with the speed of advance, it made no sense to stop, bearing in mind the distance yet to be covered to Arnhem and the river crossings ahead. Another opportunity lost. The main road to Eindhoven was easy to follow, apart from the skill of the Household Cavalry in discovering routes ahead of the main armour. If need be, another regimental group could have gone ahead, to allow the tanks of the Irish Group to refuel and re-equip.

The usual 'O' Group informed us that the advance lay through Eindhoven, Nijmegen, Arnhem, Apeldoorn, and eventually to Zwolle from where we would capture a section of the coast in preparation for the landing of the American 9th Army. At the same time, we would overrun the V2 rocket bases. As V2s had not yet been used by the Germans, we did not really understand what this meant. On the face of it, this programme looked unlikely to succeed in less than a week, assuming that we advanced at the same rate every day against minimal opposition.

After two hours of sitting in the TCVs without setting off, enthusiasm began to ebb. The delay arose from the late arrival of another infantry division to take over the town. They probably had difficulty approaching up the single crowded centre line. When eventually the leading armoured

Main square in Valkenswaard with Irish Guards waiting to resume the advance

cars of the Household Cavalry passed us, together with a squadron of IG tanks, hopes rose again. But the road being dead straight and lined by thick forest on either side, the Germans had sited 88s all the way along. It was a case of shooting it out, with the quicker and straighter aim winning. One wonders whether the guns would have been there if the advance had continued overnight instead of some twelve hours later.

Finally, amidst the cheers of the townspeople, we set off. The flat countryside consisted of the usual sand and fir trees, but with more cultivation and houses. Every so often we passed a smashed German gun half hidden in the trees. With poor weather overhead, there was no air support that day (18 September). News came of the airborne landings and the hope that the crossings over the Waal and Nieder Rhein might be secured.

We were not surprised to halt near the village of Aalst. Alec detailed me to set up a roadblock on a side road beside a bridge, to guard against flank interference. The platoon clambered on to Bill McFetridge's (later killed) troop of tanks and we clattered off. The Household Cavalry in the meantime were reconnoitring an alternative route ahead to avoid a particularly well-defended stretch of road that was holding up the advance. Over the wireless, I could hear the cavalry troop commanders giving their positions, the opposition encountered, the strength of the bridges, etc. But each alternative route had some drawback. Just then, we left the village and approached our bridge.

Visualising prepared charges and fuses as we dismounted, I dashed up and, to the surprise of a group of villagers on the other side, clambered under the bridge and poked amongst the supports. No sign of explosives, nor any need as far as I could see, since the bridge seemed about to collapse in any case. Obviously tanks could not cross. I spread the platoon out in back gardens, ditches, and upstairs rooms, with the Platoon HQ in a house.

In turn, we washed and shaved, watched by an admiring household. The housewife insisted that I sleep on the sofa in her parlour, but this was no moment for sleep. Her well-meaning solicitude became so embarrassing that I fled outside on a tour of inspection. We ignored a couple of Spandaus firing from somewhere ahead but not aimed in our direction. Our artillery came up during the halt and put down harassing fire. Half a mile away a white building like a church, with a high domed roof and minarets, was being slowly pounded to pieces. Shells passed over us in a never-ending stream until we began to regard whines and whistles as part of the natural landscape like the wind in the trees or the noise of the tide.

Around midday, a burst of Browning fire swept past Platoon HQ and buried itself in the family's air raid shelter. I peered out cautiously to see what was happening, to be met by Bill most apologetic and highly relieved that no one had been hit. Apparently one of the crew of a tank climbing into his seat had trodden on the firing lever by mistake; the recognised method of entry was to step over the gun.

For hours we sat inactive, bored and yet relieved not to be in action again. I discovered that the platoon's PIAT was jammed and refused to work, not helped by its having been dropped to the ground whilst debussing from a tank at Aalst. Sergeant Ennis took it to pieces and fixed the body to a vice that he had discovered in the house. After my efforts failed to achieve anything, he persevered with commendable energy, but it was two days before he got it to work again. In the meantime, we prayed that no enemy tanks or SP guns would attack us.

In the early afternoon, whilst the battle raged further up the centre line beyond Aalst, I was occupied in a secluded corner of a neighbouring field attending to nature. There was an orchard over the hedge, with two persistent Spandaus rattling away in the distance. All at once, there came a particularly close burst of firing that caused me to take cover, just in time to see the roof of the building housing my headquarters disappear in a cloud of smoke and debris. Tiles flew in my direction, leaving a gaping hole, but the building seemed otherwise intact. Hurrying back, I passed the rear tank of the troop, a Firefly 17-pounder, which was as much in the dark as I was. Sergeant Cole emerged from the house, gazed at the damage in surprise, and said he thought he had heard something. In the end, we concluded that either it had been a chance shot from a German SP gun or a badly aimed shot from our own artillery. At any rate, nothing more happened.

By mid afternoon, the opposition in front seemed to have crumbled. Wireless messages spoke of practically a clear run to Eindhoven where we were expected to link up with the American 101st Airborne Division which was paving our way to Nijmegen. According to orders, they would be recognised by a Stars and Stripes patch sewn permanently on each arm. It was unfortunate that, at a distance, the American helmet and uniform otherwise looked similar to those of the Germans.

Bill passed on a message to me to be ready to move at five minutes' notice. I got the platoon prepared and we sat around waiting. After half an hour, the next message changed to readiness at a quarter of an hour's notice, so we removed our equipment. A third message told us to stand down, so I lit my pipe and discussed the merits of tobacco with a Dutch civilian who showed me the dried duckweed that he was forced to smoke. He nearly coughed himself sick when he tried some of my expensive Dunhill mixture. This interlude was broken by a member of a tank crew running up to say that we were required to move at once. We got ready in a rush, as I chased stragglers to clamber on to the tanks, The troop roared back into Aalst, shaking us from side to side. There we met Alec who told me I was leading platoon, but there would also be tanks in front, as well as the Household Cavalry.

Chapter 20

Eindhoven & the Wilhelmina Canal

The troop accelerated down the road at high speed, ready for trouble and get in the first or at least the second shot. The 75-mm gun in the turret was swung to face down the road at every second. The slightest deviation in the course of the tracks meant that the turret moved, perhaps only a matter of one or two degrees. Going round a corner meant that the gun followed the road, ignoring the position of the tank hull, and all this was performed by the gunner operating the traversing gear. The tank commander stood with the top of his head out of the hatch, earphones over his black beret, binoculars glued to his eyes, and occasionally bending down to study the map.

We on the outside of the tank sat like dressed-up monkeys on a barrel-organ. Every man had to hold on to something substantial with one hand, as well as maintain his grip on his personal weapon with the other hand. I usually clung to the side of the turret where I could listen to the wireless and follow the route on the commander's map, which was on a larger scale than my own.

On the road to Eindhoven, the trail of destruction was much the same as on the road to Valkenswaard. In the thick hedges running at right angles to the road might be a blackened gap some hundred yards or so away, sometimes still flaming, with an 88-mm gun on its side or an SP gun spewing black smoke. This was balanced by an occasional IG tank burning at the side of the road, seemingly turned sideways by the shot that stopped it.

On the outskirts of Eindhoven, we passed our first American soldier standing at the side of the road and holding the hand of a small child. He waved and shouted, 'Great stuff, boys.' More and more Americans appeared, strolling round the town. It was surprising to see them in an almost peacetime atmosphere. There were no barricades at main roads, machine-gun posts, anti-tank guns, or other static defences. It seemed as if the lack of opposition made it unnecessary. The Americans waved at us, cheered with the crowds, and apart from their clothes appeared to be part of the local population.

It was the people of Eindhoven that really moved us. As they heard the approaching rumble of tanks, they poured forth in their thousands, shouting and yelling with joy. At first, we roared back lustily, blowing kisses. But the noise became so terrific that it was impossible to hear yourself speak. Above the clatter of the tank tracks, the crowds screamed and bellowed. The long street was packed with people, jostling, pushing, waving, hysterical with happiness. Above their heads was a moving sea of waving handkerchiefs, hats, hands, little flags, paper streamers. No football crowd was ever like this, and I don't suppose any of us will ever see its like again. From windows and roofs, flags hung down, people leaned perilously out, their mouths moving but inaudible.

Down the centre of the street ran a narrow clear lane bordered by a heaving mass of people that swelled out in the gaps between tanks and contracted before the next tank approached. The crowds were so close that we could lean down and touch the waving hands. It was a marvel that the tank drivers, down to a snail's pace, managed to keep so straight a path without running over anyone. Little boys leaned out from the lower levels of the crowd and occasionally darted across the road to debatable safety.

As we swung round a corner, I unwisely leant out to touch the hand of a beckoning and gaily dressed girl, and promptly overbalanced as I was not holding on firmly enough to the turret. I never reached the ground because a dozen hands caught me in mid air and pushed me back on board. We eventually crept through to the other end of Eindhoven, where on the outskirts we passed the ruins of the Philips electrical works.

Rumour had it that the RAF had bombed it.

In the open country beyond Eindhoven, we drew breath again, emotionally drained by the tension and excitement of our triumphant passage through the town. None of us had realised the enormous relief of the occupied countries at their liberation, transcending the death and physical destruction that we caused in the process.

It was now early evening, with the clouds piling up and dusk approaching. We continued to rumble on through flat open country, more cultivated than the sandy heath nearer Valkenswaard. South of the little village of Son, the platoon debussed beside a picturesque windmill that fortunately contained no snipers. Word reached us that the bridge over the Wilhelmina Canal ahead was blown, meaning that we should have to wait till a new bridge was erected. It turned out eventually that, although one of the prime objectives of the American 101st Airborne had been to capture this bridge intact, it had been blown as they were actually landing.

As leading platoon (presumably of the whole GAD), I continued forward a few hundred yards to the canal where on the other bank stood a group of American soldiers with their arms full of children. They shouted across to ask what we were going to do. Some wag replied that there was a security ban on disclosing future movements. The bridge had been smashed at both ends, so that the centre lay partly submerged in the water. On our side, a squadron of tanks was clustered and presently the rest of No.2 Company came up. We strung out along the tow-path, awaiting the arrival of bridging equipment. Two small boats plied backwards and forwards with Americans, probably liaison officers. Eventually towards dark, No.2 Company was ordered to provide local protection further down the canal to the right.

I continued in the lead down the tow-path, then struck out along a track away from the canal. It led to a heavily wooded area, with fields and agriculture. Alec had told me to hold the corner of a wood shown on the map but on the ground there was no such wood. After a hurried reconnaissance in the dark, I discovered some open ground to the left and put the platoon there. Nearby, round the corner of the track, was a farmhouse, very silent and almost invisible against the background, except for one of its outhouses which had been burnt and continued to smoulder. This made me change my mind, since it was likely that, if any Germans appeared, they would do so along the tracks and not through the pitch-black tangle of trees and hedges.

As soon as the section commanders knew their areas and had started digging, I approached the farmhouse. It was shuttered up completely with not a chink of light showing. On the other hand, there was a considerable din going on inside.

I hammered on the front door which was opened cautiously by a woman who stared into the darkness with frightened eyes. Recognising my uniform, she gave a welcoming shout, dragging myself and Sergeant Ennis (covering me from behind) into the room. It was full of people, boisterously happy and the worse for drink. They had no news of Germans but were only too willing to let me have an outhouse to sleep in. A more sober member of the household lighted a path to a disused dairy which, with several exits, served our purpose well. He even brought us armfuls of straw to soften the hardness of the stone floor. In another shed alongside, we found three American soldiers fast asleep beside the remains of a large meal.

Alec arrived and summoned a troop of tanks to bolster the defences. I got them spread out where they hopefully would not endanger my platoon if firing started. Alec decided to install his Company HQ in the same dairy as my Platoon HQ. This was unfortunate. Men were tripping over each other in the dark; the stretcher-bearers laid claim to the best corner; the signallers chatted to each other over the faint glow from their wireless set, the Company Sergeant Major detailed men to dig weapon pits; the cooks busily prepared a hot meal.

About midnight, Alec woke me up to say that a German uniform and rifle had been found under a pile of sacks in a neighbouring shed. As I was supposed to have searched the place thoroughly, what explanation had I? Of course, I had no explanation at all, except that it was pitch dark and we had no torches. It appeared that the articles had been found by a guardsman using the sacking to sleep on and, finding them uncomfortable, discovered the rifle beneath. In any case, the German was nowhere to be seen and, being an unarmed deserter, was hardly a danger.

Later I was woken again by Alec who complained that, on a tour of inspection, he had been unable to find one of my sentries. I went off to check and eventually discovered the sentry half asleep under some sheets of corrugated iron. Much irritated, I cursed him thoroughly and threatened him with court martial and death by firing squad for one of the worst military crimes – asleep on sentry-go whilst on active service.

I told Alec about it and we agreed that, since there was no proof that the man was actually sleep, we should conveniently forget the matter. Sergeant Ennis, obviously shaken by the enormity of the crime, and by regard for a man who was otherwise a good soldier, assured me next morning that the man had not been asleep but had simply failed to hear me speak. I was far from convinced. Not unnaturally, there was no further trouble with sleepy sentries. Sadly, the man was later killed in action.

In the early morning of 19 September, we tramped back through the cold mist from the canal and formed up near the wrecked bridge. Its place had now been taken by a shining new Class 40 Bailey bridge, built during the night by the Royal Engineers. Groups of weary Sappers stood round drinking cups of tea, their eyes half shut with tiredness; one man was asleep against a pile of spare girders. But all bore that self-conscious happy look of someone who has done a good job.

The Grenadier Group now took the lead. A tall Military Police sergeant resplendent in a red cap that was so 'set-up' that the peak lay flat over his nose directed traffic over the bridge as my platoon watched. Armoured cars of the Household Cavalry led the way, followed by tanks and half-tracks of the 2nd Battalion Grenadier Guards. Because the bridge could stand only a limited strain, no more than one vehicle at a time was allowed across, with vehicles speeding over to avoid causing unnecessary delay to the traffic piling up behind. It was an inspiring sight to see the armoured cars, scout cars, tanks, jeeps, trucks and Bren carriers rattling over the bridge. The shattering thunder of a 17-pounder Firefly tank travelling at speed over a Bailey bridge, with every point of the bridge reverberating, was something to remember.

In the midst of this continuous stream of armoured might, a jeep slipped through to stop beside us on the canal bank. A lanky officer stepped out, dressed in corduroy trousers, chukka boots, beret, open-necked shirt, battledress top, and a blue-spotted neckerchief. Alec standing beside me saluted. On the principle that he must know something I didn't, I followed suit, only then noticing the red tabs on the officer's lapels. It was Lieutenant-General Horrocks (Commander, 30 Corps) come to see his troops and perhaps to display the latest style in North African military dress.

The General walked out to the middle of the road, to wave on the tanks. Most tank commanders quickly sized up the position, stood up in their turrets, and saluted. This was splendid stuff, more like a victory parade than a send-off to battle. The General looked pleased and gaily despatched several tanks together on to the bridge which creaked ominously. At this, the Military Police sergeant who had discreetly stepped aside when the General had appeared leapt forward and, at some risk to himself, stopped the next tank, taking over proper traffic control. The advance was saved. For one awful moment, it had looked as if the Grenadier tanks might find themselves at the bottom of the canal with the remains of the original bridge. That Military Police sergeant deserved a medal.

The news from Company HQ was that we were due to enter Arnhem, where the airborne forces were not faring as well as hoped. It was up to us to reach them as quickly as possible. But there was nothing much that my platoon could do to help. We simply did what we were told to do and waited for orders.

As the mist cleared off the canal, the Irish Group in turn crossed the bridge behind the Grenadiers, with the 3rd Battalion in TCVs, making for St Oedenrode and Grave. It was flat country, with fields and houses on the side of the road in the usual ribbon development. At midday, we halted in a little village beside a group of American airborne, who spun hair-raising stories of the German Tiger tank that had attacked them on the night before.

The Americans carried automatic weapons of every shape and size;

none appeared to be armed with a single-shot weapon like the British rifle. They were interested in what we carried. One man offered to swap my .38 Smith & Wesson pistol for a spare automatic that he carried, simply because he had never seen one before. I pointed out that the Smith & Wesson had once been an American police issue and that, as we did not carry spare ammunition for his type of automatic, it would be shortsighted for me to swap.

The route now became littered with airborne paraphernalia. In the flat fields either side, gliders lay at all angles. Parachutes gleamed in the hedgerows, easy to pick out in their yellows, oranges, browns, blues and greens. Two Dutch farm carts were piled high with parachutes, the Dutch drivers shouting and waving to us. More and more Americans appeared by the wayside, whilst the signs of battle were increasingly evident, with shell holes, spent cartridge cases, and damaged buildings. Whenever the convoy stopped for a few minutes, my platoon (except the Bren gun sentry in the roof hole) would leap out and race for parachutes. It became quite fashionable for officers to sport a coloured neckerchief in place of the usual green camouflage net worn round the throat in place of a tie.

Chapter 21

Nijmegen

Although you would have thought the earlier arrival of the American airborne would have taken the edge off their jubilation, the Dutch people were still overjoyed to see us. Apart from the usual cheering, at our various halts they brought us presents of ripe fruit. That day I must have eaten a dozen apples, a handful of plums, and a couple of pears, as well as innumerable tomatoes.

By early afternoon, we were moving faster, crossing several intact bridges, including the big one at Grave over the river Maas, captured by the American airborne. Here, surprisingly in an American area, we saw a handful of British airborne in camouflage smocks sitting in weapon pits beside Bofors guns. The bridge bore the marks of battle, with great holes torn in the metal superstructure and in the roadway itself. In places, the TCV hugged the side of the bridge, allowing us to lean out and look through the holes down to the river far below.

Late in the afternoon of 19 September, we entered a built-up area some miles outside Nijmegen. In front, the Grenadiers were reported to be having a stiff fight to capture the town. The Irish Group behind were halted, with vehicles nose to tail for miles, unable to move forward on the single road of advance until Nijmegen was secured. This might take hours.

In relays, we washed and shaved in nearby houses, by courtesy of the occupants. It was a pleasure to remove the dirt. If possible, we washed and shaved every day, primarily to keep up morale. A man can feel happier and more alive in his reflexes when he has shaved, cleaned his teeth, and run a comb through his hair. Unlike Normandy, where we lived in the open country, the period of the breakthrough and advance usually lay through enough built up areas to allow us to use facilities in local houses where occupants were only too pleased to help. The Belgians and Dutch people were truly generous in their response to groups of dirty soldiers tramping through their houses. More often, it was a case of borrowing a basin and some water, with ablutions taking place out of doors.

The owner of a house invited me in to drink coffee, made of acorns. He was a dark sallow Dutchman with hollow eyes, newly released from prison, and speaking excellent English. Together with the rest of the platoon, we were given bunches of grapes to eat. The family said that food was scarce, although they had a fair amount of fruit now, but there would be nothing for the winter. The most acute shortage was fuel for cooking and heating, with clothing a close second.

Alec came up with urgent orders to move the men off the road. At that moment, a German plane roared low overhead and loosed off a couple of bursts of fortunately inaccurate machine-gun fire. The plane was followed closely by an RAF fighter and the pair disappeared in seconds. More aircraft came and went at great speed. For days, the sky had been empty of anything but clouds. Now, suddenly, it seemed full of aircraft, but in our part of the convoy we never came under real air attack. This was the only occasion that I actually saw a German aircraft. The RAF had almost complete mastery of the air in this sector. If anything, the speed of advance was such that the convoy was perhaps more at risk from the RAF than from the *Luftwaffe*. For this reason, the top of every vehicle in the convoy carried an identification strip.

In the late afternoon, the convoy moved forward a few more miles, still between rows of houses. At our halting place for the night, I was ordered to cover a track on the right running off in the direction of Germany which, at this point, lay a couple of miles distant. The platoon was spread out round a potato patch and a maize field, facing a mile of open ground that ended in a steep ridge covered with a thick pine forest. Miles ahead, we could hear the thunder of guns and the roar of explosives.

A troop of tanks took up position behind us in the rear of an enormous thorn hedge where they were invisible at five yards range, nor could they see us. Two 6-pounder anti-tank guns were sited behind one of my sections, making it advisable to keep heads well down. Sergeant Ennis announced that he had at last succeeded in mending the Piat. It had not so far been used and we welcomed an opportunity to test it, although I hoped it would not be me who fired it, as on the last occasion in training I had been deaf afterwards for a couple of days.

I placed Platoon Headquarters in a bungalow, occupied by a stout matron with a cheerful smile. Her feet were hidden by two or three bashful little children clutching her apron and gazing wide-eyed at me. When I commented on the children, the lady called them up and presented all nine to me, one by one. Next, the husband was summoned and it was explained that he was one of nineteen children. Finally grandmother, who was stone deaf, was ushered in, proud of her eighty-four grandchildren. We reckoned it was time for bromide in the tea.

Towards evening, a convoy of office trucks appeared in the field opposite. Alec said it was Corps HQ. A small wireless mast was set up, tents were erected, people came and went, and there was an air of bustle. In the late evening, a huge fleet of Stirling aircraft passed overhead en route for Arnhem, where the latest news was that the British airborne were in a bad way. The night passed uneventfully, but I took a poor view of the noise from the HQ's wireless trucks and the flashes of light every time someone went in or out of the tents through the black-out curtain. It was one thing for them to give away their position to enemy shelling; it was quite another to involve my platoon too.

The morning of 20 September passed with no incident. We stayed where we were, watching Dakotas and Stirlings passing over in a never-ending stream towards Arnhem. Sometimes they came with gliders, but always they went back fewer than they came. Once a Stirling was seen burning furiously and slowly falling to pieces before it finally dived into the ground, leaving two parachutes floating above it. A formation of fighter aircraft passed low overhead. Watching through binoculars, I saw a large black object detach from under a wing and come hurtling towards me. Yelling

Irish Guards manning 6-pounder anti-tank gun at the approaches to Nijmegen road bridge: a guardsman is having his hair cut

a warning, I leapt into the nearest slit trench. The platoon was startled by my action, not understanding that a bomb was supposed to be on its way. It turned out to be an auxiliary fuel tank.

The road down the centre line continued to be packed with vehicles moving up towards Nijmegen. The IG tanks behind us left to join the Grenadiers in the town. Eventually, the IG tanks lined the south bank of the Waal near the power station, to provide smoke and covering fire for the incredible assault crossing that the American 101st Airborne made over the huge river. The Americans wirelessed from the other side that they were in position at the north end of the bridge. The Grenadiers took this to mean the road bridge, when in fact it was the railway bridge some distance away. In the event, a group of Grenadier tanks rushed across the road bridge and stopped on the road beyond.

In the late afternoon, the 3rd Battalion IG was ordered to move into Nijmegen. I bade goodbye to the prolific matron with all the children and assembled the platoon at Company HQ. We all felt that trouble lay ahead. Ever since that prolonged halt on the Escaut Canal after the capture of Joe's Bridge, opposition had been piling up ahead of us. It was ironic that we were now going to Arnhem to help the 1st British Airborne which was originally intended to help us. The boot was on the other foot.

We waited interminably at Company HQ, as Alec was still attending an 'O' group at Battalion HQ. Eventually, as the first signs of darkness drew on, we moved off in TCVs towards Nijmegen. I lost track of where we were, surprised that we seemed to travel a lot further than I had thought the river would be. We passed groups of Grenadiers and Americans, muffled up against the cold, the only living beings on the streets which were otherwise deserted.

Here and there, houses were burning furiously, as they had in Valkenswaard when we first arrived. With no streets lit, we really depended on the fires to see the way. The streets were broad and tree-lined, with dark shadows under the trees, debris lying about. Not a soul to be seen in the eerie darkness. At one roundabout, we halted and the scout car leading us confessed itself lost. I stationed Bren gun sentries whilst John Stanley-Clark studied the map. A shot-up German wagon on the side of the road was apparently full of office papers, now strewn about the vicinity. It was hard to imagine who felt it so important to take a load of paper in a fighting retreat.

A vehicle was heard approaching up the road towards us. I beat a hasty retreat out of the line of fire, tripping over strands of fallen wire, but the vehicle turned off down a side-road. When at length we moved off again, the wire tangled itself in the vehicles' wheels, forcing us to detour over the pavement and round trees. In a wide street where almost every third house was burning, we met Alec, looking worried. Orders required the company to cross the bridge as quickly as possible to reinforce some self-propelled guns which had somehow gone over and now found themselves without infantry support.

My platoon was to lead the way behind Alec in the company's Bren carrier; the driver did not look too happy about this. We debussed from the TCVs which were delighted to withdraw, being rather far forward for soft-skinned vehicles. We formed up under the trees with sections on different sides of the road and men spread out five yards apart.

The only shelling was some distance away and the sound of Spandaus and machine-gun fire was quite faint. The darkness was splashed with the light from the many fires, reflected off windows and sides of houses. The crackling of flames and our own whispering were the only close-up sounds.

When Alec was ready, we led off up the road at a fair pace, with the noise of the carrier tracks reverberating off the buildings. I followed behind the leading section, catching up the section commander every now and again to make sure he had not lost contact with the carrier which was speeding ahead faster than our walking pace. Finally, we turned left and there ahead was a low horizon with no buildings to obscure it. In a ditch to the left lay a heap of bicycles, presumably German. Ahead the superstructure of the bridge towered high up in the sky. Far off on the opposite bank were flashes of light and more burning houses. A few shadowy figures of American airborne appeared, warning us to watch out for German snipers amongst the girders.

The carrier still ground on ahead, the noise changing as it moved from solid ground to the spans of the bridge. We passed concrete blockhouses and a few dead Germans. Behind me, Sergeant Cole gave a cry of joy, as he lugged a pistol from the holster of a body that I had stepped over trying to avoid a pool of blood. In the centre of the bridge, which is several hundred metres long, where the superstructure was highest and snipers most likely, a handful of Americans kept watch. They were busy coaxing a nervous German from a hole in one of the caissons, encouraged no doubt by a body tipped over the side past him and landing with a splash in the current below. On the far side, a concrete anti-tank obstacle occupied half the road, with a tall tower beyond it. A wrecked German staff car lay on the side of the road, its doors hanging open.

There was still no firing and the whole business seemed simple. The river bank on the far side was so low that the roadway continued on an embankment for perhaps another couple of hundred yards before gradually sloping down to ground level. A short distance beyond, we met the tanks of the 2nd Battalion Grenadiers who had rushed the bridge, and a troop of SP guns – 17-pounder anti-tank. The crews were inside the tanks and hardly murmured as we passed. I instructed them on no account to fire at anything until my platoon was properly dug in, as the blast would probably kill us if we were above ground.

Alec had halted beside the SP guns whilst I continued another 100 yards to set up a road-block. At this point, the road was very broad, with a line of trees down the centre, ending opposite a church. I placed a section either side of the road and one in the middle. Platoon Headquarters went into one of two adjoining houses, all empty, and found itself the latest of a series of occupants. In the front room was a bloodstained mattress and a glass of cognac on a table, a German forage cap, and a pile of American revolver ammunition. Next morning a bloodstained stretcher was found leaning against the railings outside.

Within half an hour of our arrival, a group of civilians appeared. With Glendinning, my servant, I set off to search the houses whilst the sections were digging in. It would be unfortunate if daylight found us under German fire from these buildings. A section of anti-tank guns had now come up to position themselves round the platoon, taking some time choosing their disposition.

A Dutch civilian told me that there were a couple of German motor cycles round the corner. Their bulging saddlebags provided, *inter alia*, a silk scarf, a pair of enormous fleece-lined leather gauntlets, a box camera with new film set at exposure one, and a rubberised overcoat with fancy epaulets. I kept the camera to take action photographs of war, but never had the chance. The remainder of the items were handed over to grateful Dutch civilians.

Before midnight, a civilian sedan car with headlights blazing came roaring down the road. We had some trouble stopping it, to find it full of irate American airborne. After that, we made no effort to stop the numerous requisitioned cars that passed up and down.

In the early hours of the morning, the hitherto faint and desultory sound of small-arms fire became louder and closer. It turned out to be American patrols making sure of things. The promptitude with which they opened fire at anything vaguely suspicious was startling. Patrols of Americans, wearing rubber-soled boots that made no sound, kept passing through us, alert and eager to engage the enemy. For our part, we just sat in our positions all night.

Also, in the early morning, we were shelled heavily and accurately. The Germans seemed to have pinpointed our position, although I failed to understand how, since the land was flat and we appeared to be under observation from nowhere except further down the road, and that was presumably cleared by the Americans.

Platoon Headquarters retired to the cellar for a hurried breakfast. Shells continued to rain down outside until I despaired of the remainder of the platoon surviving. High explosive shells landed in the road, against the sides of houses, and in the gardens. There came a whistle first, becoming louder and louder to reach a crescendo before the explosion. As our house shook to its foundations, the next shattering crashes rang out. After a gap of perhaps a few seconds, it all began again, some nearer, some further away, but all equally devastating. There was something inescapable about a shell. It gave so little warning and it exploded so horribly, with its smell of cordite, its scarred ring of impact, and its dreadful effects on unlucky victims.

During a lull, I had a quick look outside for casualties. Fortunately, there was nothing worse than one of the PIAT men a little shaken after a shell had pushed in the parapet of his slit trench. The soil was so sandy and collapsible that any kind of heavy movement near a trench caused the sides to fall in. Sergeant Ennis took a poor view of the PIAT man seeking better shelter away from his post, so he was sent back there. I then discovered that the carrier for the PIAT bombs was damaged, where shell splinters had torn open holes in the bombs and exposed the explosive. Luckily, the projector itself was undamaged.

Not all the neighbouring houses had been searched during the night. I took the opportunity of the lull to have a look. Piled up in the porch of a large villa, apparently used as a German store, were boxes of British 36 grenades, painted grey, with a German fuse. There were British labels in the boxes, too. Inside the house were stick grenades, egg grenades, spare machine-gun barrels and belts of ammunition, binoculars, spades, shovels, and prepared charges for demolition.

Poking about there reminded me of a similar occasion in Bayeux when, after much speculation, I concluded that one unusual object in a German dump could only be a gas-mask for a horse. It consisted of two plastic tubes, wide at one end and tapering down to a bulbous point at the other end. The two tubes were joined side by side and about four inches apart by a piece of strong tape, with further straps and buckles at intervals. There were holes in the tubes which contained a series of baffle plates. It looked as if the bulbous points of the tubes were pushed into the horse's nostrils and the whole strapped round its head. I wondered what horse was so docile as to submit to such treatment.

The house also contained a huge stock of food which the Dutch civilian population took over. There were packets labelled 'Golden Gate, Kentucky brand cigarettes' with a German seal. I could not imagine how American cigarettes could be in Nijmegen on 21 September 1944, but they were received with open arms by the platoon which had long since given its personal ration to civilians by the roadside.

As no orders had reached me, I went down the road to Company HQ which was nearer the bridge. Here there was great activity, although the firing along the river bank had ceased. A large pool of blood in the road marked where a German had been shot during the night. A signaller on duty had seen him emerging from a house and had shot him; an unusual experience for a guardsman seldom expecting to use his rifle.

As far as I could discover from HQ, the town of Nijmegen was fairly well cleared of enemy, but there were still pockets of Germans holding out on our north side of the river, notably to the right where an American battalion was dealing with them. The situation at Arnhem remained desperate. Yet the GAD did not move.

Chapter 22

Wounded

Back at my platoon, I pottered about. Sitting in a slit trench, there is little to do but clean weapons, write letters, and adjust one's legs to a less uncomfortable position. In a house, however, there is always the building to be examined and lines of fire to be decided. A German telephone in a front room appeared to be dead but gave me an electric shock when I lifted the receiver. Thereafter it became a source of amusement to draw someone's attention to the telephone and watch their reaction when they dropped the receiver in a hurry. This was far removed from proper war.

Various items of armour and Household Cavalry passed by us in the direction of Arnhem, but so far the general advance did not seem to have begun. From the radio of a scout car that had stopped in front of Platoon Headquarters came news that a body of Germans was reported to be surrendering somewhere on our right in the American sector. I decided to walk round the platoon and pass on the news to the men. I chatted to Sergeant Phillips and his section on the other side of the road and then started back, stopping to look at a pile of German grenades in the middle of the dual carriageway under one of the trees lining the centre. At that moment, there was a deafening explosion behind and almost underneath me. For a second I was dazed. Looking down at my legs and seeing the mess at my right leg, I exclaimed, 'Oh, my foot's blown off.' Below my right gaiter, there was practically nothing. A few pieces of skin and flesh hung off it. In front on the roadway, most of a bluish foot (minus the boot) lay on its side. I was aware of the most terrible pain in my leg, like a band of red-hot metal biting into my ankle.

I was still standing up on my left leg. Because more shells started to fall nearby, I swung round and hopped over to a slit trench a few yards away. Guardsman Johnston, a Bren gunner, who had been standing about five yards behind me, moaned and said, 'I've been hit, sir.' His blouse was open and there was blood on his chest and arms. I took no notice but continued hopping to the trench. He got in first and crouched at the bottom, so that as I lowered myself on the side and slipped down, my bleeding leg landed on top of him. He had apparently not noticed that I, too, had been wounded. When there was a lull in the shelling, Johnston got out and ran off, presumably to Company HQ and the Regimental Aid Post.

Standing in the slit trench, waves of pain overcame me, causing me to lose control of my mind before returning to sanity and a rational course of action. For some time, I had carried a phial of morphine in my pocket, for myself or any member of the platoon needing it. (Only officers were allowed to carry morphine; in this case, I had earlier removed the phial from a dead German.) I took out the tin, removed the cap and plunged the needle into my left forearm, feeling no pain although I had to exert pressure before the needle would go in.

On the other side of the road, Sergeant Phillips shouted to ask if I was all right. I did not answer at first but eventually roused myself enough to say I was far from it. I knew that morphine from a phial may take up to a quarter of an hour before having any effect. It was, therefore, necessary to get through that waiting period and not pass out. After that first look immediately following the explosion, I never looked down at my leg again, nor did I even apply a field dressing, so probably bled fairly heavily.

The shelling continued spasmodically as I stood in the trench, but fortunately most of it further up the road. I shouted weakly to my Platoon Headquarters for help, having an eye on the bloodstained German stretcher lying against the railings. But everyone must have been down in the cellar, as there was no response. How long I stood there, I don't know.

The matter was resolved by the Company jeep driving up (presumably alerted by Guardsman Johnston). Two stretcher-bearers doubled over, pulled me out of the trench, and laid me on the stretcher. Two shells landed fifty yards away in the road, frightening me so much that I sat up and tried to get back in the trench. Corporal Russell, a big burly man, held me down whilst Corporal Carroll put on a field dressing, both oblivious of any danger. At my request, they carried me over to the shelter of Platoon HQ, past the Household Cavalry troopers in the scout car staring curiously at me.

In the passageway of the building, the two stretcher-bearers finished tying a shell dressing on my stump and applied a tourniquet. It was five minutes past eleven, I know, because I took the time to ensure that the tourniquet was not left in position for more than fifteen minutes. Sergeant Cole appeared and I asked him to bring me my small pack. Instead, he brought my beret and cap star, which was not at all what I wanted. I bade the platoon farewell and passed a message for Sergeant Ennis, platoon sergeant, 'to carry on'. I was no longer in charge.

The stretcher-bearers took over, carried me off, strapped the stretcher to the mounting at the back of the jeep, and at my request stopped at Company HQ where Alec Hendry came out to see me. I apologised to him, knowing the difficulties he would have with only one surviving platoon commander (William Harvey-Kelly). He looked serious but remembered his part sufficiently to ask for the return of my WD watch. Both of us forgot the binoculars round my neck and the pistol in my pocket. No doubt the compass and maps with my pack and equipment in Platoon HQ were later recovered.

In this fashion, we parted. At this point, the morphine must have started to act, as my mind grew torpid. On the other hand, the pain had not lessened. Having crossed the long expanse of the road bridge, we reached the Regimental Aid Post beside Battalion HQ. I recall seeing Peter Doyle (in charge of rear link wireless) and a group of Dutch civilians standing round watching the trickle of casualties.

I have no memory of it but, when I met Corporal Russell many years later, he said that, to avoid losing the Company's stretcher, he had carried me in his arms from the jeep into the RAP, en route passing the CO who had enquired which officer had become a casualty. In the RAP, Doctor

Thynne greeted me with concern. He was a dry, long-faced Scotsman, given to lengthy anecdotes in the Mess but highly proficient in his profession. It must have been upsetting for him to meet his fellow-officers coming through on stretchers, the same men he had talked to in Malton and Eastbourne. He looked at my leg and decided to leave the dressing alone, as there was nothing he could do. Just as he was about to give me an injection of morphine, I told him I had given myself one already. He reduced the dose accordingly.

I shook hands with Corporal Russell and Corporal Carroll before my stretcher was loaded into an ambulance. Johnston was there, this time bound up with a large expanse of bandage over his front. We exchanged mutual enquiries that dwindled as I became drowsy. A few other soldiers entered to sit in the back of the ambulance, together with a medical orderly who watched me closely as if I was about to die. I was probably as white as a sheet. Presently he asked if I would like to take my steel helmet off – I was still wearing it – and was not a little surprised when I removed it myself.

The Advance Dressing Station was much like the Regimental Aid Post – a bustling room full of trestles, orderlies and doctors. The doctor who looked me over asked, 'Are you in pain?'

I was lying with my eyes shut, rather dazed, trying to withstand the pain, but at once opened my eyes and said, 'I'll say I am.'

My deepest thanks go to that doctor, for he at once gave me a small injection of Pentothal. For the first time, I felt that sensation of numbness creeping up from the inside of my elbow to my head. Before I became completely unconscious, I heard him say that I was going to an American airborne hospital as there was no British one yet in Nijmegen. I also heard him say that I had small wounds in my back.

I woke up to realise that my stretcher was being carried across a courtyard outside a large brick building. A harassed American asked me a few questions about myself and must have thought me a mental case, as I could only mumble that I was an officer. This was a pointless remark, since the hospital made no distinction between ranks. It may be imagination but I seem to remember yet another injection. Then there was a long blank and a twilight period of restlessness before I awoke with a start.

I was lying on a bed and it was late afternoon. The medical orderly came over and asked me how I felt. I must have been very truthful, for he gave me a sleeping tablet. I was lying fully dressed, even to the boot on my left leg. So Joe (or was it Al?) took it off, also my tunic which he laid across me. My leg ached intolerably. It was tied in a sort of framework which rested at an angle of forty-five degrees on the rail at the end of the bed.

The sight of my limb suddenly stopping short a few inches above the ankle renewed my feeling of utter hopelessness. I felt dreadfully tired and bewildered. Illness tends to come gradually, so that at least there is some warning of prostration. But for a normal, healthy person to be struck down in midstream can be devastating. So much had happened to me in one day. First I was strong, able and active. In the twinkling of an eye, I was reduced to a potential cripple, hardly able to move a muscle and certainly unable to think coherently. Sleep, the season of all natures, took my cares away. I remember more injections during the night and swallowing handfuls of pills.

Chapter 23

American Airborne Hospital

The morning found me more in a proper frame of mind. It was 22 September, nearing the end of the Arnhem affair. From the other Americans (all airborne) on my left and right, I gathered that this field hospital was a former maternity home near Nijmegen, converted to its present use only a few days before. There were, I think, five of us in beds facing a row of windows. Later, the spaces between beds were taken up with cases on stretchers. We were all more or less fully dressed, except the man on my right who had a ring of sticking plaster round his stomach. Each man had a single German blanket, and it was fortunate that the weather was still comparatively warm; at any rate, I never felt cold. But I do remember that the blanket was of a singularly odd shape so that whichever way round I placed it, I could never cover my left foot and my chest.

During the morning, a number of Dutch women came in to wash our face and hands. They also served the food which was nearly always a thin, watery soup with pieces of macaroni in it. It appeared, to my surprise, that the Dutch supplied the food, despite the privations of the German occupation. As none of them spoke English, it was not possible to converse. In time, it became apparent that the routine of looking after the ward was roughly divided between the orderly and the Dutch girls. He looked after the medical needs and was always on call, whilst the girls handed round the food and did the washing.

Our room must have been for serious cases. All the other occupants had stomach wounds except for one with a compound fracture of both legs. I was the only British patient. Conversation was limited as no one felt like it. But the man on my right (from Philadelphia, Pennsylvania) told me his story, roughly as follows.

'He had been detailed to relieve a machine-gunner and, whilst doing so, a body of Germans appeared in front. Gee, he had never seen a target like that before, so he must needs stand up and fire his machine-gun (an awkward thing to do, I would have thought). His pal told him to get down but, gee, he'd never seen a target like that before, so he continued to stand and fire. A return burst caught him in the belly. As he lay writhing on the ground, his more prudent colleague remarked, "I told you so".'

That was the story of a man who now regretted his action. He was never comfortable but was forever moving round his bed like a dog in its basket, sometimes even kneeling on all fours till the orderly told him to lie down. The others are just blurs in my memory, except the newly arrived stretcher case below me on my left. He appeared to be shot through the chest and was unconscious most of the time or in the process of having another blood transfusion. They could not find his veins and must have opened up much of the poor man's forearm with all the false jabs.

The daytime medical orderly was a capable, dark-haired fellow, very kind and quite master of the situation. I was the only officer in the place but rank is immaterial amongst the wounded. There were one or two British soldiers in the other room, so he told me, and we would be evacuated as soon as our own Casualty Clearing Station became available. But, at the moment, no one could go anywhere as Nijmegen was cut off by an enemy column across the centre line from Eindhoven.

No one knew anything about the battle situation; we were all more interested in our own cases. Every four hours, we were all given a penicillin injection as well as large sulphonamide tablets; after swallowing four of them, I never felt hungry. The hours of the day passed slowly, with nothing to do but sleep and worry about oneself. I lay on my back, immobile, with my right leg up in front of me, aware of ever-present pain and anxiety for the future. The surgeon who had dealt with me came to see me and said something about changing the dressing soon.

In the evening, the orderlies changed over. The night one was a tall, fair-haired man, perhaps not so proficient with the syringe. Both of them were free with the morphine. Each patient received one dose a day, and sleeping tablets quite frequently, although this was of limited use with penicillin injections every four hours. Although I normally hate injections, these two orderlies were experts at painless jabs. In British hospitals, I soon learnt that there was no such thing as a morphine injection, and in any event needles appeared blunter.

During the night I was too hot, so the orderly took my pullover off me. It struck me then that my back did not appear to have any dressing on it, nor did the case history at the end of my bed mention wounds there. When a young doctor appeared next morning, I asked him to look at my back. He sat me up, whereupon my head spun round and I had to be propped up. Dressings were placed on holes either side of my spine. I complained also of a pain in my bottom, at the top of my right thigh. The doctor heaved me up, grunted, looked again, rooted in my hip pocket and produced my revolver. I had been lying on it for nearly two days. So I unloaded it and placed it under my pillow, it being my only possession, and accompanying me back to Britain.

The framework on my right leg looked like a snowshoe consisting of two metal bars running down from my thigh, one on each side, and ending in a joined 'U' at the end. It was strapped tightly to my leg; too tightly, in my opinion, and I surreptitiously loosened the straps every now and again. Around the end of my leg was wound a lot of bandage, finishing up with a double strand of tape that stretched out over the metal loop at the end of the snowshoe. Through the double strand was a piece of wood that had been twisted over and over, to make the bandage over my stump exceedingly tight. The purpose of this, so the doctor assured me, was to draw the flesh down over the end of the bone. I took a poor view.

Later in the morning, when the surgeon appeared, I reminded him about changing the dressing having visions of a festering wound and gangrene.

'Oh, yes,' he said. 'Pete, go get the vaseline gauze.'

As soon as the surgeon had undone the tourniquet arrangement and the outer bandage, I realised I had made a mistake. It is sometimes better to bear those ills we have than fly to others that we know not of. This was definitely one of those occasions. The general ache of the severed bones gave way to the most dreadful waves of pain that quite overcame me. The bandages in contact with the severed end were soaked in blood that had dried on the exposed flesh and nerve endings. Each layer of bandage came off separately and was worse than the last. I moaned and clutched the sides of the bed. Blackness rose before my eyes and then receded, leaving me conscious again. Eventually, I lay quivering and panting with my leg disclosed. It ended just above the ankle bone and was swollen out with red raw bulges of flesh on each side of the guillotine amputation.

Having eyed the whole proceedings dispassionately, Pete now handed over the vaseline gauze which was wrapped round the stump and the whole thing was bandaged up again. They left me more dead than alive. The other patients murmured sympathetically and expressed their thanks for having nothing worse than holes through the belly.

Chapter 24

British Casualty Clearing Station

Time weighed so heavily that it was almost necessary to count the seconds. Through the window in front, I could see a dark background of fir trees. Down in the courtyard below (we must have been on the first floor), I could hear the coming and going of vehicles. The orderly said that all the British patients would be evacuated soon, but no one could be sure, as a convoy of ambulances bound for Eindhoven had turned back on the previous night when it ran into a party of Germans.

Every time someone passed the end of my bed, I winced in anticipation of their knocking against the traction splint. I tried to write a letter but had no envelope, and there was unlikely to be any post anyway. I lost the letter somewhere; it probably joined the two bullets from my revolver that eluded me as I was unloading the gun. The man in the corner with the compound fractures persuaded a Dutch girl to shave him, but declared after a look in a mirror that he was in two minds whether to apply for another Purple Heart. The remainder of us stayed unshaven and never wanted a bedpan. The medical orderly told me he had strained his back in Normandy when his glider crashed heavily. Furthermore, during this Arnhem operation, my surgeon had parachuted by mistake in the direction of Germany, requiring lengthy evasive action to reach safety.

Three whole days passed, marked only by the fact that my penicillin injections ceased after forty-eight hours, although the tablets continued. On 24 September, a tall sergeant who had hitherto busied himself with diet charts for the stomach cases came in with a stretcher for me, 'On your way, bud'. But the task of shifting me from the bed to the stretcher was well-nigh impossible, as most of the floor space was taken up by the other stretcher cases. A fat, pasty-faced doctor with rimless spectacles solved the problem in a second by telling me peremptorily to move myself on to the stretcher. Someone held up the splint whilst I inched myself across with much groaning.

In the passage outside, I lay for a few minutes beside a Coldstream Guardsman. His face was drawn, with a look of utter resignation and helplessness. He said he had been shot through the testicles. We were loaded into an American ambulance of the type where the stretchers hang from the roof on leather straps. My head was just over the driver's and he began by telling me not to smoke as he didn't want ash in his hair. It was a short but uncomfortable trip to the British CCS.

The guardsman was in agony when we were lifted down. We lay on the floor inside the entrance of a large brick building which I later learnt had been a girls' school close to the road bridge in Nijmegen. An elderly woman in khaki, with the three stars of a captain, took the usual particulars. It was the first English woman I had seen in two months, but it was unfortunate that she found it necessary to cheer us up with loud cries and facetious jokes. We were not in a mood to appreciate it, least of all the Coldstream Guardsman.

When I was carried into the operating theatre, the doctor was concerned at my extreme pallor and hoped there was some blood in me. He decided to remove the traction splint, because British medical practice treated amputations differently. Whilst delighted to see the last of the splint, I was alarmed at the thought of interference with my leg, remembering the pain of the last dressing change. The doctor calmed me down by agreeing to do the job after a Pentothal injection.

I woke up again slowly. As my head cleared, a trousered female nurse came over and said in tones of pity, 'I'm afraid you've lost your leg.'

She was not a little surprised when I shouted back, 'Oh, I know that. It's been gone four days.'

This time I was stark naked in a bed with two German blankets. It was a large room, an officers' ward, with beds all the way round.

The other occupants were a mixed lot. On my left was the Support Company Commander of the Dorset Regiment, with a wound on his knee. He had been asleep in his slit trench by the Nieder Rhein when a splinter from an airburst shell had hit him. On my right was a lightly wounded infantry officer who tried unsuccessfully for two days to get his dirty hands washed. Opposite was a Canadian pilot with a double compound fracture of one leg and something else wrong with his arm. He spent his time moaning for morphine (unsuccessfully, of course), interspersed with periods of the most enlightened witticisms. Of the others, I don't remember much.

The pain in my leg had decreased after the removal of the traction splint, but there was still a chronic ache which sharpened whenever the limb was moved. The stump was now bandaged and covered on the outside with sticking plaster that extended above the knee, so that my whole leg was kept rigid. In fact, it was over three weeks before I was able to bend my knee again. I persuaded the nurse to put a pair of pyjamas on me. Getting the trousers on took some effort and was not helped by the nurse saying that, after five days, my leg should cease to hurt. She was a bossy unsympathetic person, with no bedside manner and a habit of telling an orderly to do things. In contrast, another slender pale girl who came in occasionally worked hard, was kind and helpful, and did as much as the orderlies. She had apparently been married to an RAF pilot on the day before my arrival at the CCS.

I had not long been in bed before a series of explosions coming from beyond the trees visible through windows reminded us that the war was still in progress. It was a battery of our own guns firing at long range, and therefore presumably medium or heavy artillery. Air raids started up, too. We could hear aircraft overhead most of the day. As darkness fell, air activity increased, tailing off near midnight when the full moon was brightest and enemy bombers too obvious. The first German jet-propelled fighters appeared (all other aircraft were at that time radial-engined), with a new and distinctive sound to ears accustomed to the throb of propellers. On my second day, the air raids were particularly bad. We could hear the bombs exploding and sometimes even the whistle.

It appeared that the Germans were bombing the road bridge most of the time, an occasional bomb being aimed at the artillery battery nearby. With commendable attention to duty, the gunners used to continue to fire even when enemy planes were overhead, much to our alarm in case stray bombs came our way.

From the noise, it was apparent that there was a sentry armed with a Bren gun stationed near our windows. He spent his time firing at enemy aircraft, opening up before the Bofors anti-aircraft guns got into action, and continuing long after. In the ward, there were gloomy comments that sooner or later he would put a burst through our windows.

On this second night, we could hear the German aircraft flying low over the tree tops just after their bombing run on the bridge. The barrage sounded light, possibly because the heavy anti-aircraft guns had not yet arrived. As the objectionable nurse attempted to distribute a meal, we heard a German plane approaching very close.

The noise outside was frightening and we all lay silently in bed, conscious that we were helpless on the first floor of a prominent building near the bridge. The nurse did her best to look unconcerned but no one else spoke a word, all listening with their faces upturned. A string of explosions crept closer. When the plane was nearly overhead, we heard the bomb coming. The nurse got down under my bed, and I put the pillow over my head. The rattling and roaring passed over and exploded with a shuddering crash in the garden. We heard later that it had hit an emergency hut full of wounded.

With all the air raids, we slept little at night and less during the day. After six days, I was still in Nijmegen, within perhaps a mile or so of where I had been wounded. Apparently the road south was still cut. By the third day in the CCS, rations were reduced to a quarter of the normal, supplemented by captured German food. But I was not hungry and ate hardly at all. The officers' ward was full; remaining cases lay on their stretchers in the corridors. We could hear a very Oxford accent outside shouting occasionally for an orderly. This orderly, as nearly all of them, belonged to the Pioneer Corps and was extremely elusive.

Administrative arrangements seemed to be weak in the unusual conditions. An RAMC corporal complained bitterly that, with the staff at his disposal, he could get nothing done. Seeing an RAMC regimental sergeant major, I suggested that he should organise some local Dutch help, in the same manner as the Americans had done in the field hospital where I had earlier been. He said he would see about it, but nothing happened in the few days I was there.

None of us ever required a bedpan but we did need urine bottles at frequent intervals. Some wanted morphine, sleeping tablets or their blood transfusion apparatus altered. One person would shout for the orderly, then the rest would join in with a rousing crescendo. But seldom a sight or sign of the orderly. Instead, there was a constant noise from the floor above, where the Pioneers lived, crashing about with hobnailed boots on concrete floors. The stampede when a plane came close had to be heard to be believed.

On the night of 26 September, a member of the medical staff came round to say that a limited convoy would set off in the morning, but only of sitting-up cases. At this, everyone tried to sit up; some clearly could not make it, and I did not even try. In the end, only the Canadian, the Dorset officer, a new arrival, and myself were left in the ward, feeling very left out and despairing of seeing England again.

There was some speculation on what exactly evacuation meant. The Dorset officer thought that only a wound like mine would lead to a return to Britain, whilst he would be kept in a general hospital somewhere in France. This pessimism was disturbed by the most terrible shrieking from outside, accompanied by sounds of a struggle. It turned out to be a Polish paratrooper recovering from an anaesthetic, to find himself with a leg missing. He had torn the dressings off and was crawling off to fight the Germans again.

A similar disturbance was caused by our new arrival. He had been brought in unconscious and was now passing through a violent episode as he recovered consciousness. At one moment, he complained of being cold, then of the pain in his leg, then of the heat. The objectionable nurse had a vigorous time trying to hold him down, as he was a big man. When he was fully conscious again, to our surprise, he sat up, apologised for the commotion, and gave us the latest news of the airborne epic at Arnhem. He was a glider pilot, from Dublin, and had survived the battle until hit in the thigh by a mortar splinter whilst waiting his turn to cross the Nieder Rhein at the final withdrawal. We learnt that the airborne operation had failed and that the remaining members of the 1st Airborne had been withdrawn. This news caused discussion amongst us of the reasons for the failure but with no conclusion as we simply did not know enough about what had happened. I will presently set out my own views.

The four of us left in the ward were unhappy. It was 28 September, a week since I had been wounded. The Canadian kept asking for morphine which was refused, leading to a stream of pungent remarks. The glider pilot recovered sufficiently to take a lively interest in the prospect of evacuation. That night, when the light was turned out and there was only a candle burning in the middle of the floor, the news spread verbally that a convoy would go through on the morrow. We were agog with excitement and hardly heeded the air raids at all. I had a bad nightmare, hearing the clank of German tanks approaching and yelling for the guardsman with the PIAT to get ready. The Dorset officer quietened me down. Strangely enough, I have never since suffered a nightmare about war.

Although we were woken early, presumably to prepare us for the journey, nothing happened and the hours passed in the usual boring way. With interruptions to the long vulnerable supply line, rations were so low that breakfast at 6 am consisted of less than half a mug of tea, a small piece of dry bread, and a little German sausage which seemed to be dried blood and breadcrumbs. It looked as if we were down to captured German rations.

Finally, things began to happen. We were each given our medical particulars in an envelope from which trailed two pieces of string to be tied round a pyjama button. After the loss of my small pack, my personal belongings consisted of what was in my pockets when wounded, plus revolver, binoculars, and beret. These odds and ends of maps, pencils, wallet, cigarettes, matches, and identity discs were stuffed into the map pocket of my battle-dress trousers which had been cut out to make a temporary hold-all; even the metal stars from my shoulders were included.

I also discovered later a deep cut in my left thigh, presumably caused when someone was cutting off the trousers. The scar is still with me.

We chatted excitedly but grew despondent when nothing had happened by 9 am. It was my eighth day in Nijmegen. Then there came bustling sounds outside in the corridor and footsteps approaching. We all shouted loudly for the orderly. The door opened and, to our astonishment, in came a German soldier. He clicked his heels, bowed, saluted, and did everything bar wash his hands. For one moment, we feared we had become prisoners. More German soldiers arrived and, under the vociferous directions of the hearty nurse (who spoke not a word of German), we were transferred to stretchers, more through the efforts of the patients and the German soldiers than the nurse's directions.

The journey down the stairs was enlivened by my starting to slide foot-first off the stretcher which was tilted downhill. A lot of shouting put this right. Coming out into the open air and feeling the autumn breeze on my face was a tonic. The courtyard was full of Germans, with hardly a British uniform in sight. It turned out that the Casualty Clearing Station had originally been a German dressing station which had stayed behind when their troops withdrew earlier in the battle.

In the ambulance, the Dorset officer, the glider pilot, a Polish paratrooper, and myself waited impatiently, with the stretchers slung on rails, two on either side, one above the other; mine was on the bottom on the right. After about a quarter of an hour, we moved out on to the road, to halt under a thick cover of trees. The doors at the back of the ambulance were open, so we could see out. It turned out to be quite cold, more noticeable perhaps because we were at a low ebb and had been indoors for some time.

Overhead the usual air activity had developed from a general into a particular strafe. The driver told us that the peculiar engine sound was that of the new German jet-propelled plane (ME 262) which none of us had seen or heard before, this being probably the first operational jet. Warming to the subject, the driver went on to say that an ambulance further ahead in the convoy had suffered a direct hit from a fragmentation bomb. Hence the halt under the trees, lengthened because a patient had lost his case papers.

Eventually we got going, with much stopping and starting. Each jolt, each gear change caused my leg to bounce on the small pink cushion laid beneath it. My leg was painful and ached throughout the trip. We drove at a moderate pace, past a never-ending stream of traffic in the opposite direction. As it obviously had first priority up the road, we were several times forced to stop at narrow points. Gradually the convoy of ambulances became split up, until at length our vehicle was travelling on its own. This had the advantage of allowing the driver to choose his own speed.

Through the little window connecting the rear with the driver's cab, the Dorset officer, who was the most active of us, gave a running commentary on where he thought we were. It was left to me, as the only person who had travelled up this particular centre line before (the others had advanced on different lines), to pinpoint our exact whereabouts. We recognised the bridge over the Maas at Grave and bits of the road to Eindhoven.

After an hour and a half, I smelt burnt cordite, that overpowering stench which hangs about immediately after a shell-burst. In the next second, four explosions rocked the ambulance to one side. We all sat up in alarm. A convoy of trucks was halted along the side of the road, two of them on fire. As more 88s crashed down short of the road, our ambulance was waved to a halt and an anxious voice asked us to take on four casualties. Our driver said that we were already full up and drove off rapidly, although it might have been possible to squeeze in a couple of sitting wounded on the floor in the centre.

We in the back did not argue, although the refusal to help looks on reflection to have been selfish and uncooperative. The four casualties must have cursed as they saw the ambulance drive off without them. I wondered why a convoy of vehicles under accurate shell-fire should stop on the side of the road, presenting a sitting target, instead of driving off at speed with a good chance of avoiding the next salvo. Our own driver later told us his speedometer reached 62 mph.

We continued uneventfully and fell asleep. I awoke later to find the inside of the vehicle thick with exhaust fumes. The glider pilot closed the side window but still the fumes came in through the open ventilators. The driver explained that the exhaust pipe was carried up the outside of the vehicle to the roof to allow the vehicle to travel through water, but unfortunately the exhaust discharged almost opposite the air holes into the interior. A lamentable design fault. At midday, I recognised the Bailey bridge over the Wilhelmina Canal at Son just north of Eindhoven and the point where my platoon had dismounted from tanks for the night after the hold-up at Valkenswaard and Aalst.

Chapter 25

The Move to Eindhoven and Brussels

Compared to the cheering reception we had received when riding the first tanks through the city at its liberation, Eindhoven this time was sombre and undemonstrative, more concerned with the problems of food and shelter as winter approached. We passed through the town and turned off into the suburbs.

In the long drive of a country house, we joined a queue of ambulances. Nothing happened for three-quarters of an hour. It was now near two o'clock. At length we were unloaded and the stretchers laid out in the front hall of a large building. Busy RAMC officers and men hurried backwards and forwards, taking particulars, directing the removal of stretchers, and trying to cope with the large numbers of casualties that had suddenly arrived. A padre wandered round chatting to those who looked receptive; I was not.

We lay for what seemed a long time in that front hall, with a strong smell of stew coming from a nearby doorway to remind us that we had had nothing to eat for a good while. No one in charge told us what was happening. We lay patiently like dumb animals, not feeling well and expecting that the machine would somehow take care of us. No matter what your rank and former responsibility, once wounded you surrendered your active life and became a parcel moved about and ministered to by another organisation which thereafter had virtually complete control of your life.

From the odd stretchers being taken away, it seemed that we were splitting up to go to various places. I was taken back to an ambulance where, exhausted, I fell asleep. After about an hour's drive, I looked out of the back of the ambulance which was turning round. The doors were open because my stretcher (the fifth one) was on the floor, preventing the doors from being closed. To my amazement there was an aircraft in front of me. The other patients, all strangers to me, took no interest. I was instantly in a fever of excitement at the thought of a possible flight back to England by nightfall.

We were unloaded from the ambulance with commendable speed and laid out in a large marquee. As the first out of the vehicle, I was placed at the back of the tent, sheltered from the strong breeze blowing across the airfield but obviously at the end of the queue for flights. Those in charge of arrangements were Canadians, wearing fancy variations of the official uniform but charming, helpful, and very willing to talk.

The stretcher case on my left wore a plaster skull cap. He told me that he had been originally wounded in Holland in one arm but, whilst in the CCS at Nijmegen, a German bomb had wounded him in the other arm, his head, and chest which was now encased in more plaster. Despite that, he was cheerful and chatty. I learnt that he had served in Normandy in an infantry battalion that had failed to live up to the standards expected of it and, upon its dissolution in disgrace, he had been drafted elsewhere. This was the first I knew of the episode.

We lay for about three hours on the edge of that airfield. To my dismay, I found that we were not being flown to England but only as far as Brussels. The delay was caused by the few aircraft available and the limited numbers of patients they could carry on each trip. One of the Canadians remarked that I looked a bit thin and was horrified to hear that I had had nothing to eat since six o'clock that morning. The others, I gathered, had eaten the savoury stew I had smelt in the front hall at Eindhoven. The good man at once produced biscuits and later there was half a mug of tea all round.

At long intervals, a few stretchers would be taken out to a plane which we could hear ticking over in the background, but the queue seemed slow in reaching me at the back. As it grew dark, my turn came up to enter the plane. The process was difficult as the door opened at right angles to the direction in which the stretcher would eventually lie. Each stretcher had to be turned ninety degrees as it entered through the narrow doorway and then be hooked up in a double-tier. Mine was the last stretcher in and lay on the floor unstrapped with the stretcher above just clearing my nose by a bare three inches. The Canadians had warned us beforehand that the planes were Harrows, old type models full of struts and braces and only recently converted to their present use.

This was the first time I had flown, not that I could see a thing lying on my back in a narrow, confined space. The wind whistled through the plane which vibrated in the air and rattled ceaselessly. For over an hour, we thundered through the night. Members of the crew gave us a look-over from time to time. One of them was on edge, for fear that we would not reach Brussels in time for a rendezvous with his girlfriend. It irked me that there should be gaiety and pleasure in a city that I had helped to liberate and that I had had no opportunity to enjoy. That is often the lot of the front line soldier.

As we came down in the dark over Brussels airport, the crew told us to hang on tight. I clutched the stretcher above me with both hands, determined not to suffer a broken nose as well as my other misfortunes. The floor tilted alarmingly and there came a terrific crash underneath. But the plane held together (this was apparently the usual form of landing) and we rolled to a halt. As the last in, my stretcher was due to be the first to be removed. At least, that was the intention. But the heavy landing had caused the corner of my stretcher to break through the floor boards where it was now firmly jammed. It was quite dark. The workers were less than tolerant at the delay; likewise the other patients who could not be moved until I was.

After ten minutes, my stretcher was freed and an ambulance brought us to a building where an RAMC doctor asked each patient in turn whether he felt fit to continue the journey. Although I felt poorly, having been travelling since early morning with not much to eat and an aching leg, I decided to claim fitness, having noticed that those who admitted the strain were taken away, presumably to rest in some transit centre. The doctor was dubious when he shone his torch on me but I managed with an effort (and for the first time) to sit up, whereupon he was convinced.

The fit patients were taken back to the airfield and unloaded into a large marquee. Oil lamps hung from the roof and there were stoves to warm the place against the chill from the wind that whistled outside. It was my ill-luck to be placed yet again at the edge of the tent where a cold draught blew under the canvas. Fortunately, I had plenty of blankets but I was so restless, continually changing the position of my leg, that the blankets kept falling off. I could not bear any weight of bed clothes on my right leg, so covered it with only one blanket. This meant that my left foot got cold.

The issue of half a cup of tea each, together with biscuits and cheese, was very welcome. Two Women's Auxiliary Air Force nursing sisters looked after us and insisted on my swallowing the usual enormous sulphonamide tablets. A mild sleeping draught allowed me to sleep for a couple of hours, although my leg had become increasingly painful. After that, I could not sleep but was continually shifting the position of my leg. Nothing seemed to help.

It grew colder and colder. Blood had seeped through from my wound and dried on the dressing, so that, as I moved, the bandages tore themselves free from the flesh and skin. The night nurse walked from stretcher to stretcher examining patients. A few moaned in their sleep, others snored loudly. Unless the site of the wound required otherwise, we all had to lie on our backs on the stretcher. I must have spent at least a couple of months sleeping on my back before finding it possible to turn on my side.

Breakfast came early in the morning, followed by a couple of hours of inaction. I occupied the time rounding up my odds and ends of possessions which had somehow during the restless night strayed to various parts of the stretcher. My next-door neighbour, with a chest wound, was a cheerful fellow of untiring patience, indifferent to the delays.

At about 10 am, we were loaded into ambulances and driven to the operational part of the airfield. Stretcher-handling was carried out by an enthusiastic band of uniformed Belgian Boy Scouts who clung on to the back of the ambulance till we reached our plane, a Dakota, whereupon they went to work with enormous energy. The Dakota was a much more workmanlike plane than the old Harrow from Eindhoven. The interior had room to manoeuvre the stretchers, with an effective system of fastenings to secure them. I was placed on the second tier with another stretcher just above my nose, but at least I was beside a window, even if it looked out on a wing.

The engines were started and we took off. The noise was so loud that conversation was difficult. We flew low over Belgium, with nothing to be seen but hedges, fields, woods, houses. I fell asleep, wakening to a view of waves and sea below. I remembered that awful sea voyage in the other direction from Newhaven to Mulberry Harbour weeks ago and how seasick I had been.

Chapter 26

Back in England

After four hours' flying, we landed smoothly somewhere near Oxford. The organisation at the airfield was very competent and soon had us driven away in ambulances. During the transfer, I noticed a neighbouring patient who seemed to have a lot of personal belongings that he guarded carefully on his stretcher. This fortunate individual turned towards me and enquired what Division I had been with. Great was my surprise to discover that he, too, was in the Irish Guards, although we had never previously met (none of the patients was in uniform). Captain Terence O'Neill was Intelligence Officer at Brigade HQ where he had been wounded in the thigh at Nijmegen by a fragment from a Moaning Minnie. But, before the stretcher bearers had removed him, he had prudently collected his belongings together. This was more than I had done.

We celebrated our meeting by eating some grapes given to Terence at Brussels airfield, putting me into much better spirits. We were unloaded into a number of huts, with stretchers placed on trestles. Helpful motherly WAAFs brought us a welcome meal of stew and vegetables, being the first solid food I had eaten for eight days. Afterwards a Women's Voluntary Service worker filled in a postcard for each patient, informing next-of-kin of his arrival in the UK. The only drawback I could see was that the next-of-kin might not yet know that the patient had been wounded.

The patients showed a surprising degree of cheerfulness, particularly the more lightly wounded. A man opposite me was in the act of sitting up on his stretcher when there came the most alarming series of cracks and bangs from the trestle beneath him. His neighbours yelled loudly for the WAAF, followed by his next-door neighbour remarking, 'None of that 'ere, chum. You may be a paratroop, but you can't go jumping out now.'

After several hours of continence, a number of men began to feel the strain but hesitated to ask for help from a female. Finally a voice chirped up, 'I think someone here wants a urine bottle, nurse.' This was followed by a chorus of voices saying the same. The WAAF was well up to this and promptly made the rounds carrying a large tray of bottles which she offered to each person in turn with the utmost composure and lack of embarrassment. We were all new patients and had not yet learnt hospital procedure.

Several hours passed without further developments. Terence and I chatted at length, comparing notes and speculating on the future. There was really little to complain about; we had been evacuated as quickly and efficiently as circumstances allowed. There had been lengthy delays, giving rise to the usual comments. But, in the Army, one can seldom experience another's organisation without examining it critically. After nearly forty-eight hours on a stretcher, my back was in poor shape. The spine felt paralysed and the splinter wounds behind my shoulders ached interminably. It was only with difficulty that I could move my arms.

In the late afternoon, we were loaded into RAF ambulances which proved to be more comfortable and smoother-riding than the Army ones, and driven for miles through the gathering twilight to a railway siding where we were loaded on to an ambulance train. Again, it was an awkward manoeuvre to lift stretchers from ground level to the railway carriage and even more so to take us off the stretchers and place us in two-tier bunks along the sides of the carriage. With a thick mattress to absorb the jolts of the train, the bunks were comfortable and warm.

Terence lay opposite me with a talkative Pole beneath him. The latter, being an up-patient, paraded up and down the corridor. He told us he had been wounded in the head and this no doubt explained the unfortunate man's conduct. A string of unlikely stories poured out, of hair's breadth escapes from certain death, the award of the VC and the Polish Virtuti Militari, and a whole lot more. The head wound had clearly affected him mentally.

Further along the carriage, I recognised Andrew Philp of the Coldstream, who had served with me in the Brigade squad at Pirbright and at the OCTU in Aldershot. He gave me news of colleagues in the Coldstream. Our ways separated when the train eventually reached somewhere at about midnight after a lot of shunting, stopping, and starting. We were unloaded on to Civil Defence stretchers which consisted of criss-cross wires, not the canvas of military stretchers. With only the thickness of a blanket between the patient and the wire, it was hard going, particularly after a long day of travel. It turned out that we were in Worcester and would be taken by vehicle to Leamington Spa which we had already passed through on the train.

Terence and I kept each other amused in the dark (blackout restrictions in force), probably not giving enough credit to the Civil Defence workers helping with the continual midnight convoys of wounded. Our vehicle appeared to be a delivery van, driven by a woman whom we never saw in the dark. When we reached a building, the driver asked whether we were officers. When we replied 'yes', she turned the vehicle round and drove off somewhere else.

Towards 1 am we were carried into a dazzlingly bright hall in a Leamington Spa hospital by two elderly men and from there upstairs, along passages, through wards and then deposited in what looked like a greenhouse. It was a long room with roof and sides of glass; possibly a TB annexe. It was a delight to feel a bed under me, despite the night nurse pulling sheets and blankets backwards and forwards and then removing my pyjama trousers. It was several days before I could get them back again. My leg was bleeding and had soaked the dressing and bandage.

Terence, with all his possessions, was on one side of me; on the other side was a Scottish officer with a hole in his stomach and another in the back. He was compelled to sleep sitting up in front of a pile of pillows.

I was tired and slept soundly till half past five in the morning when the night nurse woke us all up, to start the routine of the day. Protests about having had only four hours' sleep were of no avail. She brought a bowl of water for washing. Having no razor, I could not shave, so pulled the blanket over my eyes to shut out the light and went to sleep again. Two nurses then appeared, tore the sheets and blankets off me, moved my leg despite entreaties to let it alone, and told me to get on with my toilet.

This was the beginning of months of hospital, nurses, sisters, matrons, of days that began at 6 am, of the chilling discomfort of bedpans, of occasional visitors, of hours of boredom, of agonising changes of dressings, operations, continual pain.

For a week after arriving at Leamington Spa, the dressing on my leg was not changed, although I asked a doctor, a matron, and a sister for it to be done. It was twelve days after the last dressing in Nijmegen that a doctor actually looked at my leg. The smell from it was overpowering. Even the Scottish patient in the next bed remarked on it. Not knowing anything about the details, I was worried by the possible onset of gangrene, and not at all impressed by the sister's statement that the latest treatment for amputations was to leave them alone at first.

It is noteworthy that, on re-amputation in January 1945, the surgeon removed the bandages to examine his handiwork on the very next day after the operation.

Perpetually uncomfortable with a leg that ached from time to time and with nothing to do but worry about myself, I was inclined to be critical and impatient. It seemed to me that the nursing staff were trained, as a first priority, to ensure the smooth running of the hospital to the satisfaction of the doctors, with the comfort of the patients running a distant second. This was no doubt an unkind misconception, stemming from my unhappiness, but it may have had some element of truth.

On the first day, after breakfast and the sweeping of the ward, a nurse came round to each patient to roll back the blankets from the foot of the bed, to expose the patient's feet. I complained that it was 1 October and quite cold. She replied that the doctor was making his rounds and liked to look at the patients' feet. In three-quarters of an hour's time when my left foot was stone cold, the doctor appeared. He looked at my case sheet (which was now hidden from me, despite the fact that I had carried it from Holland and had even made a few entries on it myself), mumbled something and passed on. The inspection of feet, whatever that was meant to be, never took place.

Like the majority of people, never having seen one, I had at that time but the vaguest idea of what an artificial limb looked like, how it was attached to the stump, and how mobile the wearer might be. Optimistically, I told myself that in about a couple of months' time, at least by Christmas, I would be on two legs again, possibly dancing. After all, a missing limb would not seem to be the end of the world, compared to some of the wounds that I had seen around me on stretchers.

No one had explained to me the meaning of a guillotine amputation. In a normal amputation, a flap of skin and flesh is left beyond the end of the amputation to be sewn up over the end of the sawn-off bone. With a guillotine amputation, the limb is cut straight across with no flap, thus exposing bone, flesh, nerves, and anything else inside. What I failed to realise at the time was that, until a flap of skin and flesh covered the end of the bone, no artificial limb could be fitted. From the time I was wounded, it took in all eight months before I was free of wheelchair, crutches, and hospital.

At Leamington Spa hospital, I eventually prevailed upon a doctor to change my dressing, fortunately with the aid of Pentothal. Later, the dressing was changed again, without Pentothal.

A few days after our arrival, a visitor was announced for Terence and myself. This was Lady Eardley-Wilmot bearing copies of *The Tattler* and *Illustrated London News*. I realised at once who she was: the mother of Anthony, my company commander killed during that disastrous attack on 11 August at Sourdeval in Normandy. Saying that she always visited any Irish Guardsmen in the hospital, she wanted to know whether Anthony had been told of the award of the Military Cross before his death. I could say only that news of the official award came after his death, but that he had probably been unofficially told beforehand. She was a fine friendly lady, who bore herself well despite the loss of her son only six weeks earlier.

My mother came from London to visit me, knowing only that I had been wounded in the leg. It was a shock for her to discover that the lower part of my leg was missing. Three girls whom I had known at Oxford also came to visit. These visits broke the monotony and stopped my thoughts dwelling too much on myself.

Terence's wife, a nurse, came to visit him, following which he was taken off to the X-ray department where he said they spent a long time locating the exact position of the shell fragment in his thigh, close to the sciatic nerve. They were not impressed when he said he could have saved them the trouble because he could put his finger on the spot; the leg hurt just there.

After three weeks, I bade farewell to Terence and was driven by ambulance for hours to another hospital at Bishops Stortford to be confined to bed for another three weeks in a large hutted ward of general cases. Although nursing staff here were more helpful and charming, I was still not allowed up. But when the nurses were away having their supper one evening, I persuaded a walking patient to push me in a wheelchair to the toilet. After weeks of bedpans, an actual WC was a pleasure. But the effort of sitting upright and getting out of bed left me trembling with weakness. Bed seems to breed a vicious circle of decay. The longer spent in bed, the weaker you become, and the weaker you are, the less chance of being allowed up.

My doctor was a Spaniard, reputedly a stomach specialist. On examining my leg, he said it was discharging pus (which I could smell anyway) and required twice daily washing with Eusol (Edinburgh University solution of lime). In the meantime, rest and quiet. And so, morning and evening, I suffered the agonies of gauze being stripped off the raw end where it had stuck fast. Water was poured over the gauze to loosen the dried mucus, but it seemed to have little effect.

One day the nurse doing the dressing said there appeared to be a piece of string caught up in the stump. After she had tugged ineffectually for some time with tweezers, I suggested that she leave the tendon alone as I might need it later. She looked quite mortified.

On another occasion, having cleared the pus away, the sister found a wad of vaseline gauze stuffed up the centre of the leg as a form of plug. It must have been there since 21 September, the day I was wounded, when I had been taken to the American airborne dressing station at Nijmegen. Despite my protests, the Spanish surgeon insisted on removing it at once, without Pentothal. It took him half an hour, with the sister sitting on my thighs and a nurse holding my leg steady, to stop my moaning and wriggling in agony. The operation left me trembling and white-faced, with patients in adjoining beds calling out in sympathy. It did not help to recollect that the surgeon's name was Quemada, half-way to the Torquemada of the Spanish Inquisition.

I now understood that I needed a re-amputation to produce a stump fit for an artificial limb. But there could be no re-amputation until the discharge of pus was cleared up. A doctor who was himself a patient in the ward recommended that I get myself transferred to Queen Mary's Hospital, Roehampton, which specialised in amputations. When I told him that I could not hear my watch ticking with my left ear, he was kind enough to produce his examining torch and peer into my earhole which he found to be inflamed, possibly as a result of blast from the explosion when I was wounded. Happily, my hearing has since not been affected.

To strengthen myself, I persuaded a friendly night nurse to allow me in the evenings to crawl out of bed and sit for five minutes in an armchair. I managed even to hop a few steps. Then, after three weeks, I was told I would be transferred to Roehampton. This raised my spirits. I had no confidence in the doctors who had so far cared for me, feeling that amputations were outside their experience.

Chapter 27

Queen Mary's Hospital, Roehampton

I arrived late for lunch at Roehampton. Before I had finished the meal, the dressing was removed and the house surgeon examined my leg. He told me, as if it was my fault, that if I expected to get better there was no point in my staying in bed; that I should have been up and about on crutches long ago; and that my stump was so raw that granulation was impossible for some time. I nearly had a fit on hearing all this, which confirmed my suspicions of the past six weeks. I was wheeled away in a chair (my first official sit-up) to the X-ray department where I was viewed from all angles, before being allowed back to bed at tea time.

The days that followed were tiring and I returned gratefully to my bed in the evenings, for I was already weakened. Paradoxically, my muscles were still strong. My left leg I exercised at all hours whilst my chest and shoulders now seemed unaffected by the holes in my back which had healed over satisfactorily. (The shell fragments are still there.)

At sessions of physical training under an instructress, I could do all the exercises and even manage a few press-ups. There might be a dozen or more of us, all amputees, sitting in a circle swinging arms and torsos. Tossing a football backwards and forwards across the ring one day, I hurled the ball at my opposite number, a double amputee above the knee, who promptly fell over on his back, having no legs to anchor him down. I was filled with remorse at failing to realise his problems.

In the officers' ward, there were a dozen or more patients, all with one or more limbs missing. It always turned my stomach to see what were strong young men sitting in wheelchairs with their trouser legs tucked up and two legs missing from above the knee. There were dozens of them, moving about the corridors, sitting in the sun outside, chatting to each other; always cheerful and still with the resourcefulness of youth.

My neighbour, a Gunner subaltern wounded in Italy and a 'double-amp' above the knee, moved himself about on his bottom with the aid of his hands. Wanting to open the sash-window behind his bed and unable to reach, he built up a column of books to the right height, hoisted himself up on the books and opened the window, watched anxiously by myself and other bed-patients. Those who could move on crutches or in wheelchairs helped the bedridden by bringing articles to them, straightening bed clothes, and generally being of use.

Until now, few of us had ever seen an artificial limb and had no idea how it was attached to the stump. The arrival one day of an amputee with an artificial leg (he needed a skin graft where a hot water bottle had burnt him in hospital in Italy) was a source of wonder, as the leg was passed round from bed to bed.

With time on our hands, most of us tended to think back on the war and turn over in our minds whether we had done the right thing. One officer, who had served in Italy, sought reassurance where an Italian partisan serving with his unit had been horribly wounded by a shell and had begged to be shot to put him out of his agony. The officer had duly shot him through the head and was now seized with doubts. We did our best to convince him that, from the description of the ghastly wounds, the officer had acted correctly and must now try to forget the incident.

We were heartened one day to see General Kippenberger walking through the ward. He was a New Zealander who had lost both legs below the knee from a mine in North Africa and was now doing well on two artificial legs.

Hopping from my bed one day to my locker, I caught my left foot on the loose edge of the linoleum. As I fell, I instinctively put out the other foot and landed with all my weight on the end of the stump. For a few seconds, I was paralysed with pain and shock, as other patients shouted for the nurse. I was helped back into bed, white-faced and shaking, with my stump bleeding for hours. The pain was as bad as the original wound from the shell in Nijmegen. The Irish sister in charge of the ward was sympathetic and did her best to help. I was given an aspirin.

Mr Perkins, the senior orthopaedic surgeon, had his own methods. His examination of a new case always began with the opening query, 'Where's home?' Followed by 'When do you want to go?' He believed in the recuperative effect of domestic rest and quiet.

In my own case, he explained that my stump suffered from a staphylococcal infection and would be subject to poor circulation of blood if left as a guillotine amputation just above the ankle. He advised a re-amputation higher up at the seat of selection (some six or seven inches below the knee), but emphasised that the decision was mine.

I was bewildered and loath to lose any more leg but had confidence in him and accepted his advice. So, after three weeks in Roehampton, during which time I learnt to move on crutches, I was taken by ambulance to my mother's second floor flat in Warwick Avenue, Maida Vale, in London. There I gradually built up strength, particularly up and down the stairs. It was amazing what could be done on crutches and the strength that it built up in arms and shoulders. There were pitfalls, too. It became second nature out of doors never to place a crutch on dead leaves or paper, or on wet manhole covers; to watch out for patches of frost or ice; to avoid blisters on the palms of the hands.

I spent six weeks at home on crutches, from November 1944 till January 1945. Twice a week, a Red Cross car driven by a girl would take me to Roehampton where my stump would be soaked for a quarter of an hour in Eusol and the dressing changed. The stump still oozed pus and showed no sign of recovery. I had difficulty sleeping at night and could not bear the weight of bed clothes on my leg. This meant stuffing the end of the bed with cushions to keep off the bed clothes. Circulation continued to be bad. After standing for a while, the leg would swell, turn purple, and throb unceasingly.

It was apparent that blood flowed down into the leg but could not satisfactorily find its way back. More than ever, I appreciated Mr Perkins' advice about re-amputation at the seat of selection. At length, I went back to him and said that I was willing to accept any risk of further infection if he would only do the re-amputation at once. I reckoned that, at the present rate of healing, it might take at least eighteen months before granulation was complete.

Mr Perkins thought the stump sufficiently recovered to take the risk. I returned to Queen Mary's Hospital, Roehampton, and made ready for the operation. A new patient was wheeled into the next bed, looking pale, drawn, and at death's door. This was Duke (Marmaduke) Hussey, a Grenadier subaltern wounded at Anzio, taken prisoner, and repatriated from a POW camp. Minus a leg below the knee, he had other serious wounds that left him lucky to be alive. But he recovered, went up to Oxford where we met from time to time, and in later years went on to become Chairman of the Board of the BBC.

On 9 January 1945, with my leg shaved and painted green, the re-amputation took place. From a recognisable limb that stopped short above the ankle, I woke up to a short bandaged stump some six or seven inches below the knee. The difference in size was alarming. I wondered whether the surgeon had made a mistake. On the day after the operation, Mr Perkins made his round of the ward and, to my dismay, insisted on removing the bandages to look at his handiwork. He pronounced matters to be satisfactory, which was not what I felt when I saw the flabby mass of green sewn-up flesh.

The ache from the sawn end of the bone was intolerable, but it gradually lessened and, in four days, I was able to be lifted out of bed and wheeled to the lavatory to escape the discomforts of a bedpan. The pain turned into what can only be described as sensations. There was a continual feeling of blood trickling down the sole of my missing foot, presumably a result of the new system of circulation. It did not really hurt; it was just disconcerting until I got used to it and could ignore the feeling.

In a fortnight I was on crutches again. On 1 February I left the hospital. But I felt drained of energy and lacking in desire to do anything but read. In March, when the swelling of the stump had diminished, I was measured for a new leg; in May I received it. The fitting room (in those days, separate rooms for officers and other ranks) was always crowded with patients at various stages in the process of learning to walk. The few limb-fitters were run off their feet and had little time to spare in giving instruction or passing on tips.

The more advanced patients tended to help the new ones with advice and comments, exchanging information and enquiring about the theatre of war and the loss of the limb. One RAF officer told me that he had been captured in North Africa and had lost his leg when the Italian submarine in which he was being conveyed across the Mediterranean had been attacked by an Allied warship. Another said that, on D-Day in Normandy, a cannon shell from a German aircraft had shattered his leg, which was then amputated on the spot without anaesthetic.

Measuring for a new limb consisted firstly of a plaster cast of the stump, from which another cast was taken to form the socket into which the stump would be placed. Then the remaining limb would be measured to ensure that the artificial leg was the right height. In those days, most prostheses were made of duralumin punched with holes to reduce weight and provide ventilation.

My below-knee limb was attached to me by a leather lace-up corset over the thigh, metal bars running either side from the top of the leg up the sides of the corset via a polycentric joint on each side of the knee. There was also a canvas strap attached each side of the leg and running up over the shoulder. A woollen stump sock was worn over the stump which naturally became very hot and sore with prolonged exertion. A stump sock wet with sweat could cause a blister and an ulcer. I learnt from fellow-patients in the fitting room how to reduce chafing by placing the cut-off foot of a lady's nylon stocking over the stump under the woollen stump sock.

There appeared to be fewer arm amputees than those with missing legs. This presumably resulted in part from the explosions of shells and mines having greater effect low down on the legs than on arms. It was also noticeable how many arm amputees declined to wear an artificial arm but preferred to carry on with the remaining arm and the stump. It usually meant that the amputee carried one shoulder higher than the other, because of the loss of weight of the missing arm.

A double amputation of the legs is bad enough, but an amputation of both arms is almost worse. The unfortunate amputee can do nothing for himself unless wearing an artificial arm. He can neither dress, eat, go to the toilet, or pick anything up without help. It must be humiliating to be unable, without help, to urinate or even to wipe your bottom by yourself. One of the correcting influences of a big hospital is that, however serious you may think your wound to be, there is usually some other unfortunate worse off than yourself. This can help to cut you down to size and avoid regarding yourself as a wounded hero deserving special attention.

Chapter 28

On my feet again

When I received my new leg in May, I duly stumbled up and down the fitting room between the parallel rails with a mirror either end. You took your place in the queue, with below-knee patients having an easier time than above-knee ones who had to learn to swing the leg and avoid the knee folding up unexpectedly. The possession of your own flesh and blood knee was all-important. The loss of a leg below the knee rated no more than a 40% disability for purposes of pension. Most of us were still serving in the Forces, technically on sick leave and still wearing uniform. Unless you already possessed a good wardrobe of civilian clothes, it was not possible to buy more, since we were not civilians and therefore not eligible for clothing coupons under the rationing system.

'Your gait is wrong . . . Concentrate on heel strike, roll-over, and lift-off.' 'Straighten your back' . . . 'Keep your head up and look ahead.' It sounded like the barrack square again. I had thought that learning to walk with an artificial leg would be comparatively easy. It was not. The effort and concentration required to remember with every step to brace the knee back brought beads of sweat to the brow. More than once, my knee folded up and I collapsed forwards.

Back at home, I spent hours walking up and down the street, watched by the RAF crew of a barrage balloon tethered at the lower end of Warwick Avenue. I practised up and down slopes and steps, round corners, and over obstacles. The rule was: at steps, you must take off with your good leg (leaving the artificial leg at the bottom), so that the good leg would be strong enough to lift you up to the next step. This meant adjusting your stride to arrive at the bottom of the steps with the correct foot. Over the years, my eye can now unconsciously judge several strides ahead which foot will arrive first at the steps; not that it makes any difference now, as I am able to cope with either leg.

Whilst still on crutches and bored with London, I was able to stay with Mrs Lucas-Scudamore at her stately home in Herefordshire. This good lady, with the help of her sister who lived with her, welcomed convalescing servicemen for a spell in the country in a house that reputedly had once been occupied by Owen Glendower. I was introduced to croquet, which has since become one of my delights. She was generous, always courteous, and prepared to overlook my youthful ignorance of several matters of life.

Whilst waiting at a station for the train to Hereford, a kindly lady brought me a cup of tea for which I was very grateful. When the train arrived, I was making my way slowly on crutches through the crowd, with a bag dangling on one side, when I was nearly knocked flat by a figure that barged into me from behind. Looking round, I realised it was the same lady who had brought me the tea. She was most apologetic, apparently not realising that I was moving more slowly than the rest of the mob rushing for seats in the railway carriage.

Meeting a friend who had been at school with me and was now a Royal Navy officer, I arranged for us to have dinner in the Savoy Hotel. At the end of the meal, in uniform and still on crutches, I was making my way to the entrance to try and secure a taxi (few and far between in those days) when a US Army colonel came up and offered me the use of his staff car to take me home. Much touched by his generosity, I willingly accepted and was driven by Pete or Al with great efficiency through London which he appeared to know intimately.

On another occasion, having secured a taxi and reaching home, the driver refused to accept payment. 'I served in the Irish Guards and I won't take a penny from you, sir.'

There was a lot to be said for wearing uniform and being on crutches with a flapping trouser leg. In the Guards Club one day, the only other members present were two elderly gentlemen sitting at the other end of the room. Presently they got up and came over to me. 'As former Irish Guardsmen, we'd like to introduce ourselves. My name is Godley, General Godley. And this is Gerald Munster. He used to be a Grenadier but saw the error of his ways and moved over to the Micks.'

When I reminded General Sir Alexander Godley (he had been a Divisional Commander at Gallipoli in 1915) that he had presented the shamrock to me at the St Patrick's Day parade at the Training Battalion in Lingfield on 17 March 1944, he seemed delighted. His companion, the Earl of Munster, was anxious that I should sit down, which I declined to do, having braced my knee on the chair behind me. It was a link with the past to meet two such distinguished veterans.

A further link came later in the Guards Club. Looking at *The Times* newspaper early one morning, I was surprised to find that the cross-word puzzle had already been completed. I then became aware of two elderly members behind me discussing an item in the paper about Tibet. The voice said that he had been a member of the Younghusband expedition to Tibet in 1904, when it had been necessary to spend the night at high altitude. To keep warm and avoid freezing, men had slept sitting up back to back. 'My chap's back got colder and colder. By morning, he was dead and stiff as a board.'

On yet another occasion in the Guards Club, in 1945, a group of members (myself included) were talking to an officer in a Canadian Guards regiment (Governor-General's Bodyguard if I remember rightly). Campaign medals had recently been issued. One of the members asked the Canadian what was the unfamiliar medal ribbon that he was wearing. 'Oh, that's my EBGO. Every Body's Got One. Canadian war ribbon.'

In those days, most hotels, cinemas, restaurants, and commercial houses had a commissionaire standing outside, dressed in livery. As they were usually ex-servicemen, they wore their medal ribbons. I knew my medals and frequently picked out ribbons for gallantry, apart from campaign medals for the South African War and World War I. Once I saw a Sudan medal.

By early June, I was walking slowly with the aid of a lightweight stick provided by the limb-fitting people (Hangers, a private firm). One of the girls I had known at Oxford was getting married to a British officer in the Sikh Regiment of the Indian Army. I was asked to be best man at the wedding which would take place in Oxford on 12 June, my twenty-first birthday. I did not know the fiancé, who wore an iron bracelet on his wrist; the same traditional bracelet worn by true-believer Sikhs. Apparently, the Indian officers' mess had made him drunk one night and, when he awoke, there was the bracelet on his wrist. He could not get it off, nor could he imagine how it had been slipped on. At any rate, I did my duty at the wedding, walking down the aisle with the bridesmaid.

Later in June, Robert Neild with whom I had shared a study in school invited me to go with him and his sister to the Lake District, in a car driven by his father (who had served in Mesopotamia in World War I.). It was a pleasant interlude, although I was not able to walk far over the hills. Robert was anxious to meet Professor Pigou who had lectured him on economics at Cambridge and was staying at a cottage nearby. So we walked over there one evening. Since Professor Pigou was known to be a misogynist, Robert's sister stayed outside when the rest of us entered. After a while, Robert said, 'It's just started to rain. Would you mind if my sister came inside?'

'Oh, she'll be all right in the porch,' was the reply.

Next day, whilst the others took a longer walk, I contented myself with a short trip across a hillside, en route meeting Professor Pigou, who recognised and greeted me and passed on. He was dressed in an old windjacket with pockets that had come adrift, woollen gloves that had stretched beyond the ends of his fingers and were full of holes, shoes that must have come from a rubbish dump, and an unshaven chin. This was the Cambridge professor of economics with an international reputation.

My early days of walking with an artificial leg led me unwisely to assume a gait where my disability was obvious. Having been accustomed whilst on crutches to glances of sympathy and offers of help, I became aware that this was lost when my trousers filled out and the missing leg was not apparent. But it did not take long to realise that sympathy and charity can go only so far and that in the long run it was up to me to make my own way in life as best I could, without expecting help.

In Roehampton the nurses had a deliberate policy of not doing everything for up-patients able to fend for themselves. It was not necessary to fetch and carry for them, to open doors, and generally lull them into a sense where they thought the world owed them something. Up-patients were gradually weaned to the idea that, when they left hospital for ordinary life, they must expect to do things for themselves.

In October 1945, I returned to Brasenose College, Oxford, to resume my course for a degree in law, helped by the Government's Further Education and Training Scheme which paid all tuition expenses for ex-servicemen whose attendance at the University had been delayed by the war. Almost all the under-graduates were ex-servicemen in at least their twenties, anxious to catch up on their studies and impatient with the archaic rules designed for prewar teenagers. Pubs were out of bounds; no women allowed in College after 6 pm; married men not allowed to spend the night outside College with their wives; all men to be back in College by midnight. For majors, colonels, lieutenant-commanders, and squadron leaders, all this was a nuisance, to be evaded where possible.

My sick leave expired at the end of October when I officially left the Army and was demobilised. Earlier in the Guards Club, I had been discussing with a colleague how I could get out of the Army and return to Oxford. 'Go and see Captain X in the HQ at Grosvenor Street.' I did so that very afternoon.

Captain X was at first not disposed to be helpful. 'Just because you've been wounded, you can't expect to be demobilised ahead of everybody else. A spell of PT and back to the Training Battalion with you.' He placed his arms on the desk so that I could see the wound stripes embroidered on his sleeve.

When I diffidently pointed out that with one leg I was hardly useful material for the Army, his manner changed and he apologised for not realising the position. He was as good as his word and arranged my early discharge on medical grounds. These had been set out in the two or three Medical Boards that I had already attended; in the last one I did not even have to undress.

Regimental Headquarters in Wellington Barracks sent for me one day. Colonel Montague-Douglas-Scott, the Regimental Lieutenant-Colonel, accepted that I should leave the regiment. Major Savill Young, who was present at the time, insisted that I pull up my trouser leg so that he could see my artificial leg. The Training Battalion, back at Hobbs Barracks, Lingfield, from Hawick in Scotland, also summoned me but, when I got there, the Adjutant had no idea why I had been requested. Sadly Terence O'Neill was away at the time. He died some years later without my having a chance to meet him again. After the war, he succeeded to the title as Viscount O'Neill and became Prime Minister of Northern Ireland.

I had brought my bicycle with me to Oxford, not knowing whether I was able to ride it but suspecting that it might prove essential transport. I pushed it one morning from Brasenose to the Broad which in those days was largely free of traffic. Mounting the bicycle from the pavement, I launched myself and was delighted to find that I had no difficulty in pedalling.

Owen Hickey, a fellow Irish Guardsman at Oxford, persuaded me to have a game of squash with him. He himself had lost an eye from a German stick grenade in Belgium. At first, I was all at sea, missing the ball and heavy as lead on my feet. But gradually I crept back to my former ability as a squash player.

Before long, I played regularly in the Brasenose courts with John Phillips, a former RAF bomb-aimer whose aircraft had been shot down over Germany and who had spent the rest of the war as a POW. It was a boost to my morale to discover that I could occasionally beat him, and he was no mean player. It dawned on me that I was probably capable of competing with two-legged people in many respects and that this should be my aim, instead of thinking of myself as a handicapped person condemned to a limited life.

It gradually became my unspoken philosophy to think of myself as far as possible as two-legged and to do everything that an ordinary person could do, with certain exceptions. For instance, I could not properly run except for short distances in an emergency, e.g. to avoid traffic. That meant field sports were out. I had no problem with swimming, provided

I could remove my leg close to the water's edge. This was not always easy at a beach with the tide coming in, nor was hopping in loose sand. Driving a car presented no difficulties.

Unless it was essential, I never disclosed to new acquaintances that I had an artificial leg, preferring to keep this information quiet on a need-to-know basis. This was made easier as I became better at walking, to the extent that casual observers often failed to detect anything odd about my gait, although they might if they were aware of the situation and watched carefully.

My attitude was not always shared. 'If I'd lost a leg as a soldier in the war, I'd be proud of the fact and would have no objection to letting everybody know.'

My reply was, 'If, for instance, you had artificial teeth or a rupture truss, would you go out of your way to let everybody know about it? No, of course, you wouldn't, whether it was a war wound or not. There's no need to publicise every misfortune in life. It won't put things right again, and people will pretty soon avoid you as a nuisance who seems to think that he's a wounded hero and that this entitles him to an easy passage in life.

'On the contrary, wounded heroes have to earn a living like everybody else. So it's a matter of doing your best with what you've got and not expecting any special favours. If favours come, they're very welcome, but don't expect them as a matter of course.'

As part of my philosophy of acting normally, I always wear long trousers. It irritates me to see amputees wearing shorts that expose their artificial limb. Whether they admit it or not, their purpose in doing so must be to seek sympathy; claims of keeping cool are unconvincing. Looking for sympathy is a step on the road to feeling sorry for oneself, and self-pity can destroy a person. Too often it leads to drink, which sadly is the fate of some amputees. Some leg amputees walk well and let nothing deter them, whilst others can only struggle.

It seems that walking well with an artificial leg above or below the knee and using an artificial arm depend partly on the amputee's physical state and age and partly on their mental attitude. A leg amputee who has problems with the stump or injuries to the other leg may find walking well to be a problem. The extent to which he responds depends on his will to walk. I remember being much struck by an obituary in *BLESMAG*, the journal of the British Limbless Ex-Servicemen's Association, about a former soldier who had lost a leg above the knee in World War I and had then spent his entire working life thereafter as a bus conductor on a double-decker bus, climbing up and down the stairs.

On my many visits over the years to limb-fitting centres in Britain, Hong Kong and Australia, the majority of patients have been elderly persons who have lost a leg as a result of diabetes or cardiovascular disease. In most cases, it was apparent that these unfortunates were no longer physically capable of learning to walk again properly, nor had they the mental determination to do so. Their eyes showed no promise of fight. They seemed resigned to life in a wheelchair. I have tried to show some that they can still walk again and enjoy life, but the reply has too often been to the effect 'It's all very well for you to say that, but you started walking many years ago at the age of twenty. I'm too old now to start again with a long physical struggle. I've got hip trouble and arthritis, and I'm wobbly on my feet at the best of times.'

On the several occasions that orthopaedic surgeons have examined me for the purpose of deciding whether to authorise the production of a new limb, they have tended to feel my stump and give it a firm squeeze, causing me to exclaim loudly and pull the stump away. This usually surprises the surgeon. It surprised me, too, until I learnt from a helpful Chinese limb-fitter in Hong Kong that the majority of stumps tend to shrink with age and to become insensitive. Hence the squeezing. But a minority (mine included) remain sensitive to poking and prodding.

Many wartime amputees suffer for the rest of their lives from occasional phantom pains in the nerve endings of their stump. No one appears to have yet discovered the precise reason for this, nor a satisfactory method of combatting it. Happily I seldom suffer from this, and then only after prolonged physical exertion. It seems that Mr Perkins performed an excellent job in my re-amputation. In other cases, surgeons may have tried to save as much limb as possible where legs or arms were shattered, and this may have resulted in an awkward stump.

It was fellow amputees in a fitting room who alerted me to a new system that allowed a strap round the waist instead of the former strap over the shoulder. Then later I learnt about the new PTB (patella tendon bearing) below-knee limb which did away with the leather corset up the thigh. It simply carried a strap over the leg above the knee, making it a matter of seconds to put on and take off the leg (now made of fibreglass instead of duralumin), particularly when buckles were replaced by velcro fasteners. Life is now more comfortable and I have no complaints. The British government pays me (and other war disabled) an annual disability pension and provides an artificial limb free of charge. I am happy enough to be alive.

Chapter 29

Adequate Generalship?

I am less than happy with the generalship that led to the Arnhem fiasco, though. It was many years later that I eventually pieced together what had apparently happened to cause potential victory to turn into abject failure. For some twenty years after the end of the war, I was too busy with my job and my family to bother with the wartime past. It was my wife who insisted on resurrecting my campaign medals (tarnished and still separate from their ribbons) and on my attending Armistice Day services.

Not until I retired after thirty-five years' service in Hong Kong with HM Overseas Civil Service did I start to read the several books on Operation Market Garden and the Arnhem operation. These opened my eyes. It was only too obvious that, in early September 1944, the planners had decided to use the large British and American airborne forces which had been kept in Britain chafing at the bit since D-Day. The British 6th Airborne Division and various American airborne units had been involved on D-Day, but the British 1st Airborne Division and American airborne units had not; they were now anxious to take part, particularly after a series of cancelled operations had led to a not unnatural feeling of frustration.

Hence the planning for Operation Market Garden which would consist of airborne operations ahead of the Guards Armoured Division, to capture various road bridges over the several large waterways that the GAD must cross on the way into northern Holland, including the capture of the launching pads for the V2 rockets. The aim sounded excellent. It was the unrealistic planning and the execution of it that came unstuck. My mind turned to that splendid Army Council pamphlet handed to us at the OCTU, entitled 'The tactical handling of an armoured division in the opposed crossing of a water obstacle'.

Events began on 10 September when the Irish Guards captured Joe's Bridge over the Escaut Canal at Lommel in northern Belgium, close to the Dutch border. There was no German counter-attack overnight and everyone expected the advance to continue next day against disorganised opposition. But nothing happened. We sat still. Two days later, on 12 September, Lieutenant-General Horrocks (Commander 30 Corps) came up to the bridge and announced that there would be 'no move for the Guards Division before the 16th', with the Irish Guards leading the next advance.

So, after the headlong dash to Brussels and beyond, the GAD stopped advancing for six whole days, giving the Germans ample time to organise a defence, and experience showed that they were very good at that. This was only too apparent when Operation Market Garden opened on 17 September with the leading Irish Guards tanks suffering heavy losses in the advance. The delay had arisen because the planners had decided that the earliest the airborne operation could be mounted was the 17th. No convincing reason has ever been given why the GAD could not have continued to advance from 11 September on the day after the capture of Joe's Bridge, with the airborne operation taking place from the 17th. This might have ensured a link-up at the Arnhem road bridge by the 18th, the airborne having been assured that they were expected to hold the bridge for not more than forty-eight hours.

There have been claims that the delay was necessary to allow supplies of fuel and ammunition to reach the GAD up the long thin line of communication. Was this really so? There must be considerable doubt that the GAD was unable to move another yard unless it sat around for six days. It is hard to believe that a resolute commander would not have insisted on the GAD pressing on regardless and keeping up the momentum of the hitherto rapid advance. If necessary, air drops of supplies might have been organised. Instead of that, a priceless opportunity was thrown away.

When the Irish Guards late in the evening of 17 September (the first day of Operation Market Garden) eventually reached Valkenswaard in the south of Holland, there was only minor German opposition in the town. Again, there was no overnight advance; we stayed the night there. (In fact, the GAD never to my knowledge advanced at night, although it appeared possible to do so; battles took place at night, but no advances. Night advances might have created problems for tanks but probably acceptable.)

On the following day, 18 September, the road bridge at Son over the Wilhelmina Canal north of Eindhoven was found to be blown. A Bailey bridge was erected overnight. Next morning, 19 September, I watched the 2nd Battalion (armoured) Grenadier Guards cross the new bridge to lead the advance. There was not more than twelve hours' delay; even less taking into account the fact that the GAD did not advance at night. But the bridge at Son was still over forty miles from the bridge at Arnhem, and the GAD was supposed to have linked up with the 1st Airborne by this day.

On the evening of 20 September, the Grenadiers captured the road bridge at Nijmegen, and I led my platoon over the bridge in the dark to take up a position astride the road ahead. Again, we sat there all night, with no German counter-attack. We had all been informed that the 1st Airborne were in dire straits at Arnhem. It was a moment when you would have expected the commanders to order the Grenadiers to continue hell for leather to Arnhem, with the 3rd Battalion Irish Guards riding on the tanks. Neither battalion was otherwise seriously engaged all night and should have been available.

In his book, *It Never Snows in September*, which describes Operation Market Garden from the German point of view, Robert J. Kershaw quotes German commanders on the spot as stating afterwards that, on the night of 20 September, the main road from Nijmegen to Arnhem was virtually undefended, with only security pickets reinforced by one or two outposts. For five hours between 1900 hours and midnight, the way was open for a British push northwards. With astonishing resilience, Major Knaust succeeded in improvising a Kampfgruppe which, after midnight on 21 September, started to move south from Arnhem. By dawn, a German force of over two battalions and sixteen tanks was set up on a line at Elst, roughly half-way on the fifteen kilometres between Arnhem and Nijmegen. By 1600 hours, this force had swelled to five battalions and twenty-five tanks and self-propelled guns. Against this, the GAD advanced on a one-tank front up a mostly embanked road, with little hope of deploying to the flanks.

Poor visibility ruled out air cover that day. The GAD's advance north from Nijmegen did not start till after midday on 21 September and at once ran into trouble, petering out short of Arnhem. We shall probably never know why the GAD was not ordered to continue the advance north from Nijmegen directly after the road bridge was captured. It was one of the tragedies of World War II that such a golden opportunity was lost and that the 1st Airborne were left to their fate.

It was shameful for the GAD to have sat all night on 20 September and all the morning of 21 September at Nijmegen without making any effort to reach Arnhem and help the unfortunate 1st Airborne. It seemed almost as if no one in command took the Airborne plight seriously. It is relevant to note that Lieutenant-General Horrocks (Commander, 30 Corps) was a sick man for part of the campaign in Europe and perhaps not always at his brightest. General Montgomery knew this but nonetheless secured his appointment and kept him there.

In retrospect, my conclusion is that Operation Market Garden was excellent in intention, unrealistic in planning, and poor in execution. The troops on the ground deserved better.

Chapter 30

Who was to blame?

In my view, the failure of the GAD to reach Arnhem in good time had three causes: six days' delay at Joe's Bridge; failure to advance at night after reaching Valkenswaard; failure to advance at once after capturing the road bridge at Nijmegen. And who was to blame? Generals Montgomery and Horrocks, likewise the GAD commander. They may have been excellent generals in other campaigns and battles, but in this particular instance they were far from adequate.

It is also worth querying why British armour for the Second Front was equipped with 75-mm guns when most German armour was known to carry 88-mm guns that could penetrate Sherman tanks with ease. The British had years in which to prepare for the Second Front, with North African experience of German armour and its capabilities. Despite this, British (and American) armour was armed with an inferior gun.

The British device of equipping one Sherman tank (Firefly) in each troop with a bigger 17-pounder gun was an unsatisfactory answer, because it tacitly acknowledged that the other three tanks (with 75-mm guns) in the troop were no match and in effect expendable. The proper answer might have been to equip all British Sherman tanks with a 17-pounder gun, likewise all anti-tank artillery (most anti-tank artillery consisted of 6-pounder guns). It was a sad error of judgment on the part of the planners and unfair on the crews.

Chapter 31

Operation Market Garden Revisited

In September 1994, I took part in a commemorative tour with other members of the Irish Guards Association, their wives, and widows to mark the 50th anniversary of Operation Market Garden. Some 150 of us (mostly veterans of the campaign) set off in three coachloads from Chelsea Barracks in London to Ramsgate, crossed to Ostend, and drove along excellent roads through the flat country of Belgium and Holland to Eindhoven. For this 50th anniversary, local authorities had invited whichever Guards regiment had liberated them in 1944.

On the first full day, there was a civic reception at Lommel in north Belgium, with speeches and hundreds of spectators beside the plaque commemorating the Irish Guards' capture of Joe's Bridge over the Escaut Canal. On the second day, there was a similarly splendid reception in Valkenswaard (south Holland). On the third and final day, the local authorities in Eindhoven hosted an even more impressive reception, reminding us that the Irish Guards had led the advance to liberate the city.

On each civic occasion, under the command of a serving Warrant Officer 2, the veterans marched behind a uniformed piper, to the delight of the local crowds. The obvious pleasure and gratitude of the Belgian and Dutch populations were quite overwhelming. Roadside banners read 'Welcome Liberators' and 'Your yesterday gave us our today'. We were plied with souvenirs, food and drink. It was an astonishing and heart-warming display.

The Ever Open Eye

But it was not all fun and games. Every day we visited one or more cemeteries of the Commonwealth War Graves Commission to honour Micks buried there. Wreaths were laid, the Last Post and Reveille sounded by our uniformed bugler, followed by 'Oft in the Stilly Night', the Irish lament played by the piper. Veterans paid their last respects to long-dead comrades, lingering round headstones and exchanging remarks such as, 'Do you remember Sergeant So-and-So? He was in charge of No.2 Section.'

In one speech, a local dignitary said that he had been a small boy at the Liberation of his town in 1944, but he remembered how at the Irish Guards cookhouse he and other young lads were always given something to eat (the Dutch population then was half-starved during the German occupation). He recalled how, for the first time in his life, he had tasted chocolate and rice.

In the evenings, the veterans took over the bar in the Eindhoven motel where we stayed. Notwithstanding that the youngest was aged sixty-nine and the oldest in his mid eighties, that bald heads were more common than thatch, and that stomachs tended to be generous, the Irish songs and piping lasted till early morning. There was sadness back in London when contingents separated to return to Northern Ireland, Southern Ireland, and all points in England, not to mention two to Australia.

In fact, I went back the very next day with the Grenadier Guards Association to Nijmegen, which I particularly wished to see. Since it had been liberated by the Grenadiers, it was not part of the Irish Guards tour. Two coachloads of Grenadier veterans, a dozen Household Cavalry, one Royal Army Service Corps driver (who had served in Nijmegen), and myself travelled to Nijmegen, for a week of civic receptions, parades, church services, marches, visits to cemeteries and war museums. A plaque commemorating the Grenadier capture of the road bridge was unveiled in front of a huge and appreciative crowd. The Historic Military Vehicles Club of the Netherlands drove Sherman tanks, scout cars, armoured cars, Bren carriers, and TCVs in a procession which to everyone's surprise did not break down. The Pipe Band of the 48th Highland Regiment of the Netherlands, resplendent in kilts and bonnets, gave us traditional

The Ever Open Eye

Scottish airs on the bagpipes.

Hundreds of British veterans from other regiments that had taken part in Operation Market Garden were also present. Medals tinkled and flashed everywhere. At various functions were small parties of American veterans from the US 82nd Airborne Division and from Polish units. A proposed parachute drop by American veterans (none aged less than seventy), who had trained for months, had to be cancelled because the wind speed was too high. A sad disappointment.

As far as the weather was concerned, it was always windy, cold, and overcast, raining occasionally for the Irish, every day for the Grenadiers. When we finally parted, the cry was 'I'll see you all in twenty-five years' time for the 75th anniversary. Do your best.'